my **revision** notes

Edexcel **A2**
RELIGIOUS STUDIES DEVELOPMENTS
PHILOSOPHY OF RELIGION AND ETHICS

Gordon Reid

Text credits

p.9 J L Mackie, *The miracle of Theism* (1992); **p.13** Douglas Gasking, *Ontological Arguments* (2011); **p.24** Peter Moore, *Religious Studies Review* (2006); **p.26** Melvin Tinker, 'Dawkins' Dilemmas' in: *The Briefing*, Issue 337 (October 2006); **p.27** Maurice Wiles, *God's Action in the World* (1986); **p.30** J A T Robinson, *A Handbook of Christian Theology* (1960); **p.37** Anthony Flew, *Theology and Falsification* (1955); **p.41** Dr Rowan Williams, *A dictionary of biblical interpretation* (2003); Keith Ward, *Holding fast to God* (1994); Peter Vardy, *The Puzzle of God* (1995); **p.43** Jon Nelson, *The Immorality of Religious Morality* (1996); **pp.52, 69** William K Frankena, *Ethics* (1973); **p.60** G E Moore, *Principa Ethica* (1903); **pp.66, 69** C Horner and E Westacott, *Thinking Through Philosophy* (2000); **p.68** J Macquarrie and J Childress, *A New Dictionary of Christian Ethics* (1990); **p.72** Jeremy Bentham, *Principles of Morals and Legislation* (1988).

Although every effort has been made to ensure that website addresses are correct at time of going to press, Hodder Education cannot be held responsible for the content of any website mentioned in this book. It is sometimes possible to find a relocated web page by typing in the address of the home page for a website in the URL window of your browser.

Hachette UK's policy is to use papers that are natural, renewable and recyclable products and made from wood grown in sustainable forests. The logging and manufacturing processes are expected to conform to the environmental regulations of the country of origin.

Orders: please contact Bookpoint Ltd, 130 Milton Park, Abingdon, Oxon OX14 4SB. Telephone: +44 (0)1235 827720. Fax: +44 (0)1235 400454. Lines are open 9.00a.m.–5.00p.m., Monday to Saturday, with a 24-hour message answering service. Visit our website at www.hoddereducation.co.uk

© Gordon Reid 2013
First published in 2013 by
Hodder Education,
An Hachette UK Company
338 Euston Road
London NW1 3BH

Impression number   10 9 8 7 6 5 4 3
Year   2017 2016 2015 2014

Cover photo © Irina Tischenko – Fotolia
Typeset in CronosPro-Lt 12/14 points by Datapage (India) Pvt. Ltd.
Printed in India

A catalogue record for this title is available from the British Library
ISBN 978 14441 82460

Get the most from this book

This book will help you to revise for the Edexcel A2 Religious Studies: Philosophy of Religion and Ethics specification. It is essential to review your work, learn it and test your understanding. Tick each box when you have:

- revised and understood a topic
- tested yourself
- practised the exam questions.

☑ **Tick to track your progress**

Use the revision planner on pages 4–5 to plan your revision, topic by topic.

You can also keep track of your revision by ticking off each topic heading in the book. You may find it helpful to add your own notes as you work through each topic.

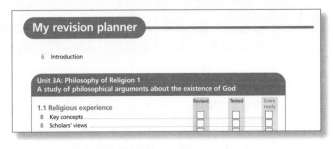

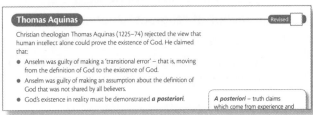

Features to help you succeed

Exam tip

Throughout the book there are tips to help you boost your final grade.

Typical mistakes

Identifies the typical mistakes candidates make and explains how you can avoid them.

Now test yourself

These short, knowledge-based questions provide the first step in testing your learning. Answers are provided at the back of the book.

Key words

Clear, concise definitions of essential key terms are provided on the page where they first appear.

Key quotes

Quotations from key scholars concisely express key ideas or views relevant to each topic.

Exam practice

Practice exam questions are provided for each chapter. Use them to consolidate your revision and practise your exam skills.

Online

Go online to check your answers to the exam questions at www.therevisionbutton.co.uk/myrevisionnotes

My revision planner

Exam practice answer guidance at **www.therevisionbutton.co.uk/myrevisionnotes**

Introduction

What is Philosophy of Religion about?

Philosophy of Religion covers some of the deepest and most important questions that have ever been asked – questions like 'Can we experience God?', 'Are religion and morality linked?', 'What happens when we die?', 'Can we speak meaningfully about God?' and 'What are the main critiques of religion and are they justified?'

What is Ethics about?

Ethics looks at the kind of people we are and what we mean by right and wrong/ good and bad. It asks question such as 'How do we choose good from bad?', 'Is morality separate from religion?', 'Why do we make the choices that we do?', 'What do we mean by law and justice?'

Philosophy of Religion and Ethics examine and evaluate questions like these. Studying these subject areas will help you to develop your own views and understand and appreciate those of others.

Studying A2 Philosophy of Religion and Ethics will help you to develop:

- an interest and enthusiasm for philosophy, religion and the wider world
- an interest in how we make ethical and moral decisions
- your knowledge, understanding and evaluative skills
- an enquiring, critical and reflective mind
- your own views and opinions

What is covered in A2 Philosophy of Religion?

Unit 3 Area A: Philosophy of Religion

1 Philosophical arguments about the existence of God:
   - Religious Experience – key ideas, strengths and weaknesses
   - Ontological – key ideas, strengths and weaknesses
   - Non-existence of God and critiques of religious belief
2 Selected problems in the philosophy of religion:
   - Beliefs about life after death: reincarnation; rebirth; resurrection; immortality of the soul
   - A study of religious language: analogy; language games; myths and symbols; verification and falsification debates

Unit 3 Area B: Ethics

1 Ethical concepts:
   - Critiques of the relationship between religion and morality
   - Deontology, natural moral law, virtue ethic – key ideas, strengths and weaknesses
2 Selected problems in ethics:
   - Meaning and definition of ethical terms with reference to 'is/ought' and debates about 'good'; emotivism
   - Objectivity, relativism, subjectivism

How is AO1 and AO2 assessed?

Candidates answer three questions. They must study two units and may not answer more than two questions from the same unit.

The external examination is 1 hour and 45 minutes. The total number of marks is 30 per question and 90 overall. The 30 marks are made up of 18 for AO1 and 12 for AO1.

For AO1 candidates are expected to:
- Select and demonstrate clearly relevant knowledge and understanding
- Use evidence and examples to explain key ideas

- Use correct, accurate and clear language and terminology
- Use relevant and accurate information
- Identify important features

For AO2 candidates are expected to:
- Critically evaluate and justify a point of view
- Analyse alternative views and scholarly opinion
- Use evidence and reasoned argument
- Express issues clearly, using appropriate vocabulary

Countdown to my exams

6–8 weeks to go

- Start by looking at the specification available from www.edexcel.com. Make sure you know exactly what material you need to revise and the style of the exam to familiarise yourself with the topics.
- Organise your notes, making sure you have covered everything on the specification. The revision planner will help you group your notes into topics.
- Work out a realistic revision plan that will allow you time for relaxation. Set aside days and times for all the subjects that you need to study, and stick to your timetable.
- Set yourself sensible targets. Break your revision down into focused sessions of around 40 minutes.

Revised ☐

4–6 weeks to go

- Read through the relevant sections of this book and refer to the exam tips, typical mistakes and key terms. Test your understanding of each topic by working through the 'Now test yourself' questions in the book. Look up the answers at the back of the book.
- Make a note of any problem areas as you revise, and ask your teacher to go over these in class.
- Look at past papers. They are one of the best ways to revise and practise your exam skills. Write or prepare planned answers to the exam practice questions provided in this book. Check your answers online at www.therevisionbutton.co.uk/myrevisionnotes.
- Try different revision methods. For example, you can make notes using mind maps, spider diagrams or flash cards.
- Track your progress using the revision planner and give yourself a reward when you have achieved your target.

Revised ☐

One week to go

- Try to fit in at least one more timed practice of an entire past paper and seek feedback from your teacher, comparing your work closely with the mark scheme.
- Check out the revision planner to make sure you haven't missed out any topics. Brush up on any areas of difficulty by talking them over with a friend or getting help from your teacher.
- Attend any revision classes put on by your teacher. Remember, he or she is an expert at preparing people for examinations.

Revised ☐

The day before the examination

- Flick through these Revision Notes for useful reminders, for example the exam tips, typical mistakes and key terms.
- Check the time and place of your examination.
- Make sure you have everything you need – extra pens and pencils, tissues, a watch, bottled water, sweets.
- Allow some time to relax and have an early night to ensure you are fresh and alert for the examinations.

Revised ☐

My exam

**A2 Unit 3 Religious Studies – Developments
AREA A: Philosophy of Religion and Ethics**

Date: ....

Time: ....

Location: ....

**A2 Unit 3 Religious Studies – Developments
AREA B: Ethics**

Date: ....

Time: ....

Location: ....

1.1 Religious experience

Key concepts

A religious experience is an encounter with the divine – an experience of God as a personal reality. It is an experience beyond ordinary **empirical** explanation and may be:

- individual and subjective – where an individual is made aware of a transcendent reality
- corporate – where a group of people appear to be influenced by powers beyond normal understanding
- ineffable – a state of feeling that defies expression.

> **Empirical** – evidence from observation.

Christian mystic St Teresa of Avila (1515–82) wrote of her experiences: 'God establishes himself in the interior of this soul in such a way, that when I return to myself, it is wholly impossible for me to doubt that I have been in God and God in me.'

The most famous example of a religious experience is the biblical account of Saul's conversion on the road to Damascus: '… suddenly a light from heaven flashed around him. He fell to the ground and heard a voice say to him, "Saul, Saul, why do you persecute me?"' (Acts 9:4).

> **Exam tip**
>
> Make sure that you can explain a range of different types of religious experience. Don't just rely on one type. The more you know, the more you will have to say in your answer, which will add to your answer's depth and scholarship.

Scholars' views

Caroline Franks Davis ———————————————— Revised ☐

In *The Evidential Force of Religious Experience* (1989), philosopher Caroline Franks Davis suggested the following types of religious experience:

- seeing the work of God when looking at the world (awareness experience)
- having a vision or other inner experience of God (quasi-sensory experience)
- encountering the holiness of God (numinous experience)
- a conversion experience (regenerative experience)
- having prayers answered (interpretive experience)
- a sense of the ultimate reality (mystical experience)
- receiving enlightenment and knowledge, perhaps through a revelation from God (revelatory experience).

Friedrich Schleiermacher ———————————————— Revised ☐

In *On Religion: Discourses to its Cultural Despisers* (1994), German theologian Schleiermacher (1768–1834) defined a religious experience as:

- offering a sense of the ultimate
- an awareness of wholeness
- a consciousness of infiniteness and finiteness
- a feeling of absolute dependence
- feelings of reverence, joy and a desire to belong to God.

Paul Tillich

Philosopher Paul Tillich (1886–1965) in *Systematic Theology* (1951) described two stages in a religious experience: an event or encounter followed by a special understanding of that event which reveals its religious significance. He said that religious experiences produce a feeling of 'ultimate concern' – a feeling that demands a decisive decision from the one receiving it.

Rudolf Otto

German theologian Rudolf Otto (1869–1937) coined the word 'numinous' to describe the experience of the holy – something that is wholly other than the natural, physical world. Often a person would see a vision and then experience a feeling of the power and majesty of God. The person may then go on to feel ashamed. In the Bible, the prophet Isaiah explains it in this way: 'Woe is me! For I am lost, for I am a man of unclean lips … for my eyes have seen the King, the Lord of Hosts' (Isaiah 6:5).

Brian Davies

Philosopher Brian Davies (b.1951) in *Philosophy of Religion* (1981) argued that the fact that not everyone has had a religious experience was not grounds to dismiss testimonies of them. He also suggested that everyone may have had such an experience, but only a few have actually realised that they have. He described such an experience as follows: 'Just as I can reasonably say that there is a bed in my room because I have encountered it, so I can reasonably say that there is a God because I have directly encountered him.'

Martin Buber

Philosopher Martin Buber (1878–1965) argued that God reveals himself to people on a personal level as they experience him in life and in the world – in other words, people experience God through interaction with other people and through nature. He called such relationships 'I-Thou'. He argued that it is in such relationships that we experience God – He is 'the Eternal Thou' (from *I and Thou*, 1970).

Typical mistake

Remember that it is not only religious believers who have religious experiences. Many **non-believers** have claimed to have had similar types of experiences.

Non-believer – someone who does not believe.

Now test yourself

1 In what sense is religious experience beyond ordinary empirical explanation?
2 What is a regenerative experience?
3 Who defined religious experience as a 'feeling of absolute dependence'?
4 Who coined the term 'numinous'?

Answers on page 75

Exam tip

Don't forget to include contrasting views of scholars in your answer. Without them, your answer will be simplistic and lack the depth and insight needed for a top grade.

Types of religious experience

A religious experience is one in which a person becomes overwhelmingly aware of the presence of God. Religious experiences have several common features:

- a profound sense of union with God
- a transcendence of time
- a clear revelation
- a sense of joy and well-being.

William James

American philosopher and psychologist William James (1842–1910) made a great in-depth study into religious experiences.

In *The Varieties of Religious Experience* (1902) he observed that religious experiences are emotional reactions directed at God. The result of such an experience will be:

- reverence
- a joyful desire to belong to God
- a renewed approach to life
- a sense of union with the divine
- a sense of dependence on God
- a sense of separateness from God
- time is transcended
- 'noetic' experiences – something is clearly revealed to the person receiving the experience
- a sense of joy and well-being.

He concluded that there were four common factors of religious experiences:

- **Ineffability** – the person experiences a state of feeling that 'defies expression, that no adequate report of its contents can be given in words.'
- **Noetic quality** – the experience provides revelations of universal and eternal truths.
- **Transiency** – the experience is brief but profoundly important.
- **Passivity** – the person feels that they are taken over by a superior authority.

James also identified what he called 'the characteristics of the religious life', namely:

- The visible world is part of a more spiritual universe.
- Union with the spiritual universe is the ultimate aim.
- Prayer is the main method of achieving this.
- Prayer aids the flow of spiritual energy.
- Religion produces psychological characteristics including love of life, earnestness and heroism.

James believed that religious experiences were deeply personal, but this made testimonies too subjective to be convincing proof of the existence of God for those who have not had such an experience. However, for those who have religious experiences, they are the most convincing proof of all: 'The only thing that it unequivocally testifies to is that we can experience union with something larger than ourselves and in that union find our greatest peace.'

However, James also acknowledged: 'The sway of alcohol over mankind is unquestionably due to its power to stimulate the mystical faculties of human nature, usually crushed to earth by the cold facts and dry criticisms of the sober hours. Sobriety diminishes, discriminates, and says no; drunkenness expands, unites, and says yes.' Mystical experiences, he therefore concluded, could also be due to the external influences of alcohol or other intoxicants.

Now test yourself

5 What is a numinous experience?
6 How did Schleiermacher define religious experience?
7 What did Martin Buber call religious experience and why?
8 What are the four common features of religious experience identified by William James?

Answers on page 75

Tested

Exam practice answer guidance at **www.therevisionbutton.co.uk/myrevisionnotes**

A special case: mystics

Mystics are those who actively seek religious experiences. True mysticism incorporates three special steps of preparation:

- **purgation** – ridding the soul/mind of unnecessary thoughts
- **illumination** – God opens the person's mind to enable them to understand about Him
- **contemplation** – the mystic feels a unity with the divine and may experience perfect love and goodness.

St Teresa of Avila

St Teresa experienced deep mystic states and claimed to have felt the presence of Jesus. In *The Autobiography* she taught of the way the soul passed through four stages to reach God:

- devotion of the heart – through contemplation on the suffering of Christ
- devotion of peace – a state of inner peace, coming from God
- devotion of union – a feeling of spiritual joy as the soul encounters the love of God
- devotion of rapture – a trance-like state in which the person has a great feeling of light and ecstasy as the soul is absorbed into God's power.

She described how the person feels that their soul or consciousness has left their physical body. In this state, they often claim to have felt a whole range of emotions such as love, pain and joy as they believe that they are experiencing a brief union with God. Afterwards, the person returns in a state of weakness and joy.

> **Typical mistake**
>
> Mysticism is a very important type of religious experience because there are many testimonies of the effects of it, which are useful in the examination (for example, Teresa of Avila). However, don't fall into the trap of thinking that mystics are all super-religious or eccentric people. Many mystical experiences have happened to ordinary people, some of whom have, as a result, gone on to become famous and acknowledged scholars and teachers. Referring to testimonies of mystical experiences could add useful depth to your answer.

In favour of religious experiences

Richard Swinburne

Philosopher Richard Swinburne (b. 1934) supported religious experiences for the following reasons:

- The principle of credulity – unless we have overwhelming evidence to the contrary, then we should believe that things are as they seem to be.
- If God is loving and personal, then he could reveal his identity to humanity.
- The principle of testimony – we cannot constantly doubt people's accounts of religious experiences.

I suggest that the overwhelming testimony of so many millions of people to occasional experiences of God must, in the absence of counter evidence, be taken as tipping the balance of evidence decisively in favour of the existence of God.

An omnipotent and perfectly good creator will seek to interact with his creatures and, in particular, with human persons capable of knowing him.

In the absence of special considerations the experiences of others are (probably) as they report them.

(The Existence of God, 1979)

- So many thousands of people have had an experience of what *seems to them* to be God that we should believe them. The sheer weight of testimony, from so many people is sufficient to prove the existence of God.

- If religious experiences have a deep effect on the life of those who experience them, then they cannot be considered to be meaningless.

- What are the grounds for claiming that the testimony of religious believers is any less reliable than that of non-believers?

Swinburne identified three types of evidence that would indicate that a person's experience is not as they report it:

- The circumstances surrounding the person make their account unreliable, for example they have used hallucinatory drugs.

- There is evidence that things are not as they are reported.

- There is evidence that the experience was not caused by God.

Now test yourself

9 What are Swinburne's principles of testimony and credulity?

Answer on page 75

Tested

Criticisms of religious experiences

The main problems with religious experiences are:

- The experiences are subjective and personal and not subject to objective testing.

- We cannot carry out a scientific experiment to determine whether the experiences are authentic.

- The experiences can be interpreted in a variety of different ways.

- Ludwig Wittgenstein talked about *seeing-as*: people mistake what they have seen or experienced.

- Moral philosopher R M Hare (1919–2002) said that a person's interpretation of experience is clearly mistaken, but they continued to hold on to it. This is a **blik**.

- If God does not exist, there can be no experience of him.

- The testimony of religious believers is questionable and cannot be counted as reliable evidence.

- Mystical experiences may be the manifestation of psychological needs.

- The emotions and sensations that accompany religious experience can be explained by biological or neurological factors.

Blik – an unverifiable and unfalsifiable way of looking at the world.

Richard Dawkins — Revised

Evolutionary biologist Richard Dawkins (b. 1941) in *The God Delusion* (2006) claimed that there is no such thing as a religious or mystical experience – they are just expressions of a person's psychological needs:

> If we are gullible, we don't recognize hallucinations or lucid dreaming for what it is and we claim to have seen or heard a ghost; or an angel; or God ... such visions and manifestations are certainly not good grounds for believing that ghosts or angels, gods or virgins are actually there.

He claimed that testimonies of mystics are an illusion created by the mind to enable people to cope with their fear of the unknown:

> If you've had such an experience, you may find yourself firmly believing that it was real. But don't expect the rest of us to take your word for it, especially if we have the slightest familiarity with the brain and its powerful workings.

Key quote

'Religious experience … is essentially incapable of supporting any argument for the additional central doctrines of theism.'

(J L Mackie)

Now test yourself　　　　　　　　Tested ☐

10　How did Paul Tillich understand religious experience?
11　How did William James understand religious experience?
12　How does Richard Dawkins understand religious experience?

Answers on page 75

Michael Persinger　　　　　　　　　　　Revised ☐

Scientist Michael Persinger (b. 1945) constructed an electronic helmet which induced 'religious experiences' by putting small electric signals and magnetic vibrations into the temporal lobes and front of the brain in the wearer. By suppressing this part of the brain, the sense of individuality is temporarily lost; the right and left temporal lobes feel separated from each other, with each part experiencing that there is 'something there' but not knowing what it is. Some people who have worn the helmet claim to have had mystical experiences.

John Hick　　　　　　　　　　　　　　　Revised ☐

In *The Existence of God* (1977), philosopher and theologian John Hick (1922–2012) observed that testimonies of religious experiences might also be equally well interpreted in non-religious ways: '… any special event or experience which can be constituted as manifesting the divine can also be constituted in other ways, and accordingly cannot carry the weight of proof of God's existence.'

A J Ayer　　　　　　　　　　　　　　　Revised ☐

In *Language, Truth and Logic* (1936), philosopher A J Ayer (1910–1989) dismissed the claims to religious experience on the grounds that although the fact that 'people have religious experiences is interesting from the psychological point of view, it does not in any way imply that there is such a thing as religious knowledge.'

Anthony Flew　　　　　　　　　　　　　Revised ☐

Philosopher Anthony Flew (1923–2010) argued that the testimony of religious believers was biased, irrational and questionable and could not be regarded as meaningful because there was nothing that could count against it. He said that religious believers were so convinced of the truth of their religious statements that they often refused to consider evidence to the contrary.

Sam Harris

American philosopher Sam Harris (b. 1967) agreed and in *The End of Faith* (2004) wrote: 'We have names for people who have many beliefs for which there is no rational justification. When their beliefs are extremely common we call them "religious", otherwise they are likely to be called "mad", "psychotic" or "delusional" … while religious people are not generally mad, their core beliefs absolutely are.'

Now test yourself

13 Why did A J Ayer reject the meaningfulness of accounts of religious experience?

14 Why did Anthony Flew argue that the testimony of believers is unreliable?

Answers on page 75

Conclusion: does religious experience offer convincing proof for the existence of God?

There is no clear-cut answer as to whether religious experiences prove the existence of God. Religious experiences are too personal and subjective to be convincing proof. However, for those who have had them, religious experiences are the most convincing proof of all. As philosopher William James observed in *The Varieties of Religious Experience* (1902): '… the results of a religious experience are the only reliable basis for judging whether it is a genuine experience of the divine.'

Key quote

'The results of religious experiences are the only reliable basis for judging whether it is a genuine experience of the divine.'

(William James)

Exam practice

Answer the following as a test essay in 35 minutes.

(a) Examine the view that it is meaningless to speak of religious experience. **(18 marks)**

(b) Assess the view that religious experience provides convincing proof of the existence of God. **(12 marks)**

Answer guidance online

Online

Summary

- ✔ An encounter with the divine.
- ✔ Beyond empirical explanation.
- ✔ Experiences are individual and subjective.
- ✔ People feel a sense of the ultimate, joy and well-being.
- ✔ There is a lot of supporting testimony.
- ✔ However, there are doubts over the reliability of testimonies.

- ✔ There may be psychological explanations.
- ✔ There may be a number of different explanations.
- ✔ There is a lack of empirical evidence.
- ✔ Religious experiences are convincing to those who have had them, but are not necessarily convincing to those that have not had the experience.

1.2 The Ontological Argument

Key concepts

The Ontological Argument:

- attempts to prove the existence of God by reason alone
- is *a priori* – an argument that does not rely on the evidence of the senses, but on logical argument
- produces a conclusion which claims to be self-evidently true or logically necessary
- is **deductive** in that the argument contains the conclusion that it reaches
- is **analytic** in that it is true by definition alone.

Anselm of Canterbury

Revised

The Ontological Argument was developed in 1078 by Christian philosopher Anselm (1033–1109) in *Proslogion*. The argument can be broken down into three stages:

1 The definition of God is '… that than which nothing greater can be conceived'.
2 The non-existence of God is logically impossible.
3 'The fool' believes that it cannot be true.

Anselm's argument is that:

- When we speak of God, we intuitively understand what is meant by the term 'God'.
- God is 'greater' than all other beings in the sense that he is supremely perfect.
- 'That than which nothing greater can be conceived' must possess all perfections.
- When we speak of God we speak of such a being.

Anselm argues:

- If such a being possesses all perfections, it must exist because existence is perfection.
- It must exist **in re** (in reality).
- It does not exists simply **in intellectu** (in the mind).
- This is because what exists in reality is greater that what exists in the mind.
- God is a **necessary being**.
- Therefore God's existence is **de dicto** (by definition).

> **Key quote**
>
> 'Without doubt, therefore, there exists, both in the understanding and in reality, something than which a greater cannot be thought.'
>
> (St Anselm)

> **Exam tip**
>
> Try not to use too many bullet points in your answers. You should always try to write in full sentences.

> **Exam tip**
>
> If you want to achieve the highest grade in your examination, don't forget that the assessment objectives for AO1 require you to offer 'a good range of relevant evidence' with 'examples deployed to show a clear understanding of the main issue(s) raised.'

> **Necessary being** – one that must, logically, exist.

Now test yourself

1 What is an a priori argument?
2 What is an analytically true statement?
3 Why did Anselm believe he had proved the atheist's position was unstable?
4 What is existence in intellectu and in re? Which is greater?

Answers on page 75

Typical mistake

This is a popular examination topic. Don't make the mistake of concentrating just on strengths – you will need to weigh them up against the weaknesses in order to come to a balanced conclusion.

Strengths and weaknesses

Strengths	Weaknesses
● It is a deductive argument.	● Not coherent – how can God be **omniscient**?
● If valid it will be proof for both believer and atheist.	● Mutually inconsistent – no being could be both **omnipotent** and omnipotent since an omnipotent being could make a creature which had a secret unknown to anyone but itself, while an omniscient being must know every secret.
● The definition of God as 'that than which nothing greater can be conceived' is accepted by the atheist, even if the atheist denies that there is such a being in existence.	● Leads to a **useless God** – so distant from religious experience as to be useless?
● The atheist must have an understanding of God to be able to reject belief in God.	● It cannot be assumed that this is the only logical way of defining God.
	● When we say that existence is part of God's definition, we are merely saying that no non-existing being can be God.

Scholars' views

René Descartes

Philosopher René Descartes (1598–1650) supported the Ontological Argument because it did not rely on what he regarded as unreliable empirical evidence. He wanted believers to realise that when they used the word 'God' they meant an infinitely perfect being superior to all beings in perfection. As Descartes could conceive of his own existence, he believed that he could also conceive of the existence of a perfect being:

1 I exist.
2 In my mind I have the concept of a perfect being.
3 As an imperfect being, I could not have conjured up the concept of a perfect being.
4 The concept of a perfect being must therefore have originated from the perfect being itself.
5 A perfect being must exist in order to be perfect.
6 Therefore a perfect being exists.

OR

1 The idea of God is the idea of a supremely perfect being.
2 A supremely perfect being has all perfections.
3 Existence is a perfection.
4 A supremely perfect being has the perfection of existence.
5 If God possesses the perfection of existence then it is illogical to think of God as not existing.
6 God exists.

Omniscient – all-knowing.
Omnipotent – all-powerful.
Useless God – a God not worthy of worship.

Key quote

Descartes famously said that the fact that he doubted himself proved his own existence: 'Cogito, ergo sum' – 'I think, therefore I am.'

(René Descartes)

Typical mistake

This is a complicated concept and candidates can get muddled up. Make sure that you assign the right arguments to the right scholar.

Thomas Aquinas

Revised

Christian theologian Thomas Aquinas (1225–74) rejected the view that human intellect alone could prove the existence of God. He claimed that:

● Anselm was guilty of making a 'transitional error' – that is, moving from the definition of God to the existence of God.

● Anselm was guilty of making an assumption about the definition of God that was not shared by all believers.

● God's existence in reality must be demonstrated **a posteriori**.

> **A posteriori** – truth claims which come from experience and knowledge.

Aquinas observed: 'The argument is only meaningful to understand the essence of God completely. Only God can completely know his own essence, so only He can understand the argument' (adapted from *Summa Theologica*).

Now test yourself
Tested

5 Why do some say that Anselm's view leads to a 'useless God'?

6 In what sense is the Ontological Argument an a priori one?

7 What does it mean to say that something is 'self-evidently true'?

8 Explain the meaning of the phrase 'de dicto' and give an example of it.

Answers on page 75

Gaunilo of Marmoutiers

Revised

French Benedictine monk Gaunilo (c. 1060) demonstrated that if the logic of the Ontological Argument were applied to things other than God it would lead to invalid conclusions. Replacing the word 'God' with 'the greatest island' leads to an argument which has the same form as Anselm's and yet which leads to a false conclusion:

1 I can conceive of an island greater than which no island can be thought.

2 Such an island must possess all perfections.

3 Existence is a perfection.

4 Therefore the island exists.

> **Contingent being** – one that depends on other things (such as food) in order to exist.

However, Gaunilo's criticism was exposed by Anselm who said that his proof was:

● intended only to apply to necessary beings, not to **contingent beings** such as an island, which may or may not exist

● not understood by atheists who have failed to understand the full implications of the concept of God.

Key quote

Can it be that there is no such being since, 'the fool hath said in his heart "There is no God" … But when this same fool hears what I am saying – "A being than which none greater can be thought" – he understands what he hears … even if he does not understand that it exists … Even the fool, then, must be convinced that a being than which none greater can be thought exists at least in his understanding.'

(Gaunilo)

Now test yourself
Tested

9 Why did the Ontological Argument appeal to Descartes?

10 Why did Aquinas reject the Ontological Argument?

11 What did Gaunilo aim to demonstrate?

Answers on page 75

Exam tip

This key quote is good but far too long to use in an examination. Try to use short, one-line quotations to support your answer.

Immanuel Kant

Revised

German philosopher Immanuel Kant (1724–1804) opposed the view of Anselm that existence was necessary for perfection. He called this a **predicate**, that is, something that can be stated as true about an object without actually seeing or experiencing it. Thus, if God had all perfections, then a predicate of God would be that he actually existed. However, Kant observed:

- Existence is not associated with the definition of something, since it did not add to our understanding of that thing.

- We must establish the existence of something before we can say what it is like, not the other way around.

- We cannot ascribe existence a priori to our definition of a perfect being.

> **Predicate** – something that is true without seeing or experiencing it.

> **Key quote**
>
> 'God is an object of pure thought.'
>
> (Immanuel Kant)

Douglas Gasking

Revised

Australian philosopher Douglas Gasking (1911–94) demonstrated the fallacy of the Ontological Argument:

- The creation of the world is the most supreme achievement conceivable.

- The greater the limitation of the creation, the more impressive the achievement.

- The greatest limitation of a creator would be non-existence.

- Therefore, a world created by a non-existent creator would be greater than one created by an existent creator.

- An existing God is therefore not the greatest conceivable being, since an even greater being would be one that did not exist.

- Conclusion: God does not exist.

> **Key quote**
>
> '… there is no need to view the creation of the world as the most marvellous achievement imaginable.'
>
> (Douglas Gasking)

> **Now test yourself**
>
> Tested
>
> 12 Why did Kant reject the Ontological Argument?
> 13 What did Douglas Gasking aim to demonstrate?
>
> **Answers on page 75**

David Hume

Scottish philosopher David Hume (1711–76) considered the Ontological Argument a failure because:

- It made a false assumption about existence – that necessary existence was a coherent concept.
- Existence could only ever be contingent.
- All things that could be said to exist could also be said not to exist.
- Existence is simply a matter of fact. No form of existence could be analytically true.
- It is not possible to move from a de dicto definition of existence to a in re existence. Only the latter is verifiable.

Key quote

'We cannot define something into existence – even if it has all the perfections we can imagine.'

(David Hume)

Norman Malcolm

American philosopher Norman Malcolm (1911–90) argued that the very nature of God meant that if he did not exist necessarily, then he did not exist at all. Malcolm proposed a form of the argument in support of necessary existence working on the presumption that if God *could* exist, he *does* exist:

- God is that than which nothing greater can be thought.
- Necessary existence is a perfection.
- If God possesses all perfections he must possess necessary existence.
- A necessary being cannot not exist.
- If God *could* exist then he would exist necessarily.
- It is contradictory to say that a necessary being does not exist.
- God must exist.

Key quote

'… existence cannot be a perfection of something.'

(Norman Malcolm)

Now test yourself

14 On what grounds did Malcolm support the Ontological Argument?

Answer on page 75

Tested

Alvin Plantinga

American philosopher Alvin Plantinga (b. 1932) furthered the argument by claiming that since God is **maximally great** and perfect, then he must exist in all possible worlds and will be the same in each one of them. He suggested that:

- We are able to imagine any number of alternative worlds in which things may be quite different.
- There must be any number of possible worlds, including our own.
- If God's existence is necessary, he must exist in them all and have all the characteristics of God in them all.
- This is because God is both maximally great and **maximally excellent.**
- Such a being would be omnipotent, omniscient and omnibenevolent in all worlds.
- In *God and Other Minds* (1967), Plantinga observed: '… the greatest possible being must have maximal excellence in every possible world.'

Maximally great – as great as possible.

Maximally excellent – as excellent as possible.

Typical mistake

Many candidates only write about Anselm and Gaunilo in the examination. Remember to include a range of these modern scholars as well to balance and give depth to your answer.

Richard Dawkins

British evolutionary biologist Richard Dawkins rejects the Ontological Argument, claiming that it is 'logomachist trickery' that 'offends me aesthetically' and should be treated with suspicion because it has no basis in empirical fact or scientific observation and lacks even 'a single piece of data from the real world'. He writes in *The God Delusion*:

> **Let me translate this infantile argument into the appropriate language, which is the language of the playground:**
>
> **'Bet you I can prove God exists.'**
>
> **'Bet you can't.'**
>
> **'Right then, imagine the most perfect perfect perfect thing possible.'**
>
> **'Okay, now what?'**
>
> **'Now, is that perfect perfect perfect thing real? Does it exist?'**
>
> **'No, it's only in my mind.'**
>
> **'But if it was real it would be even more perfect, because a really really perfect thing would have to be better than a silly old imaginary thing. So I've proved that God exists. Nur Nurny Nur. All atheists are fools.'**

(The God Delusion, 2006)

Now test yourself

15 What does it mean for God to have necessary existence?

16 Why did Dawkins oppose the Ontological Argument?

Answers on page 75

Tested

Conclusion: is the Ontological Argument convincing?

The Ontological Argument has puzzled scholars for centuries. Without the evidence and experience of the universe on which to draw, the argument needs to be analytically sound. It may be regarded by some as successful if the first premise is universally accepted. However, while 'God is that than which nothing greater can be conceived' may be true for *some* believers, it is not necessarily the case for all. The real weakness of the argument is that it lacks empirical evidence, and reason alone cannot show that an absolutely necessary being exists or does not exist.

Exam practice

Answer the following as a test essay in 35 minutes.

(a) Examine the principle themes of the Ontological Argument for the existence of God. **(18 marks)**

(b) Assess the failure of the Argument to prove the existence of God. **(12 marks)**

Answer guidance online

Online

Summary

- ✔ An *a priori* proof that relies on logical argument.
- ✔ God is 'that than which nothing greater can be conceived' (Anselm).
- ✔ God is supremely perfect and a 'necessary being'.
- ✔ God possesses all perfections, including the perfection of existence.
- ✔ God is a non-contingent being.
- ✔ However, the Argument makes God a distant figure.
- ✔ It is incoherent – God cannot be both omniscient and omnipotent.
- ✔ Lack of empirical evidence.
- ✔ You cannot simply reason God into existence.

1.3 Non-existence of God and critiques of religious belief

Non-existence of God

Atheism

Revised

Atheism means 'without/no God'. **Theism** is a belief in a personal, loving God. **Weak atheism** is the absence of belief in the existence of God. **Strong atheism** is a strongly-held belief that God does not exist.

Atheists may adopt their position for several reasons, which may include:

- There is no such being to whom the description 'God' can be given.
- All so-called experiences of God can be explained in other ways.
- Evil and suffering count decisively against the existence of God.
- Believers in God are deluded.
- Their distrust of organised religion may lead to rejection of belief in God.
- They may hate religious beliefs and believers.
- They may think that belief in God serves only to support those who are emotionally, intellectually or psychologically weak.

- Loss of faith, unanswered prayer and bad experiences of religion.

Theists are those who believe in the existence of a loving God. They argue against atheists by claiming:

- If God cannot be proved not to exist, then X must exist – if arguments against the existence of God fail, then, logically, God must exist.
- If God cannot be proved not to exist, then God may exist – failure to disprove the existence of God does not render his existence necessary, but it is probable.

Agnosticism

Revised

Agnostics claim that it is not possible to know whether God exists or to know the nature of God. An agnostic may well claim to be open to knowing about God, but is unsure how to recognise this. It is possible to say that **agnosticism** is merely another form of atheism. Agnosticism is essentially concerned with the problem of what we can genuinely know.

Listed below are a few other perspectives in note form – make sure you know these basics:

> **Typical mistake**
>
> Many candidates think that non-believers and atheists are the same thing. Be careful – an atheist considers the evidence and chooses to believe that there is no God. A non-believer is simply someone who does not believe in God, but may not have made such a serious decision, based on evidence, that the atheist has.

Materialism:

- The only things that exist are energy and matter.
- All things are composed of matter.
- Reality is the reaction of different types of matter to each other.
- Matter is primary.
- Mind and spirit are secondary because they are the result of matter acting with other matter.

- There are no supernatural or immaterial things.
- Therefore, there is no God.

Naturalism:

- The laws of nature operate the universe.
- Nothing else exists except the natural universe.
- There is no purpose to nature.
- There are no supernatural things.
- Therefore, there is no God.

Scepticism:

- There is probably no such thing as certain knowledge.
- Belief in something does not mean knowledge of it.
- No certain belief is possible.
- No truth is completely knowable.
- Therefore it is impossible to know God.

Non-belief:

- If God is all-loving, he would want everyone to believe in him.
- If God is all-powerful, he could have ensured that everyone believed in him.
- But, some people do not believe in him.
- Therefore, God does not exist.

Unbelief:

- Unbelief is a lack of faith or a rejection of religious belief.
- Author Salman Rushdie wrote in 'Imagine no heaven' (2006): 'To choose unbelief is to close out dogma and to trust in our humanity, rather than all these dangerous divinities'.

Critiques of religious belief

Critiques of religious belief examine the role of religion in society or in people's lives and tend to conclude that religion creates social and hierarchical structures which have a powerful effect on the lives of individuals and communities. Critiques of religious belief tend to reach the conclusion that 'God' is the name given to something else, such as 'society'. In turn, religious beliefs are seen as maintaining a social structure of benefit to some but not others, and preventing the individual from realising the full potential of their humanity. Indeed, some critiques say that religious beliefs deceive people as to what is truly real.

Key quote

'If you exclude the supernatural from science, then if the world is supernaturally caused, you won't be able to reach the truth scientifically.'

(Alvin Plantinga)

Sociological critiques: Emile Durkheim

Revised

French sociologist Emile Durkheim (1858–1917) offered a functionalist theory of religion in which he claimed that religion unites and preserves the community. He defined religion as:

> **A unified system of beliefs and practices relative to sacred things ... beliefs and practices which unite into one single moral community called a church, all who adhere to them**
>
> (*The Elementary Forms of Religious Life*, 1912)

Durkheim saw religion as:

- one of the forces that creates within people a sense of moral obligation to follow their society's demands
- belief that is expressed in shared rituals, values and identity, discouraging change
- projections of the power of society.

Durkheim wanted people to follow a non-religious morality based on the recognition that we are what we are because of society.

Exam practice answer guidance at **www.therevisionbutton.co.uk/myrevisionnotes**

Criticisms

- For religious believers, although membership of the religious community is important, their primary loyalty is to God.
- The theory does not explain how religious believers are sometimes prepared to go against the norms and laws of society.
- Durkheim's thesis was modelled on primitive aboriginal societies, and is not a true reflection of modern religious belief.
- While society constantly changes, beliefs about the nature of God are timeless and unchanging.

Now test yourself

Tested ☐

1 What is a critique of religious belief?
2 What is the difference between strong and weak atheism?
3 What was Durkheim's view of religion?

Answers on page 75

Karl Marx

Revised ☐

German philosopher and economist Karl Marx (1818–85) argued that:

- God was an invention of the human mind in order to satisfy emotional needs.
- The rulers use religion to dominate and oppress their people, offering them an illusion of escape.
- Humanity created God.
- Religion is an alienating force, giving to a non-existent God powers that humanity in fact possessed.
- Humanity has lost control over their own destiny through belief in God.
- Only by loving one another rather than God could humanity be truly free.
- Religion offers a false promise of release from distress.

Criticisms

- Religious beliefs and teachings can be open to interpretation.
- Religion can be an influence for both change and stagnation.
- While some religions may appear to discourage change, others encourage it.
- Religion is no longer necessary in a capitalist society and yet it still exists.

> **Key quote**
>
> 'Religion is the sigh of the oppressed creature, the heart of a heartless world … it is the opium of the people.'
>
> (Karl Marx)

> **Typical mistake**
>
> Don't fall into the trap of thinking that arguments against the existence of God and critiques of religious belief are the same thing. They are not – the first is about God, the second is about faith.

> **Exam tip**
>
> Remember that when you are answering part (b) examination questions, you are being tested on your evaluation skills. To get the highest grade you will need to offer 'a coherent response in which scholarly opinion and careful analysis support a critical evaluation of the issue(s) raised.'

Now test yourself

Tested ☐

4 How did Durkheim define religion?
5 How did Durkheim understand the function of religion?
6 Why did Karl Marx believe that humanity invented God?
7 Explain why Marx used the phrase 'opium of the people'.

Answers on page 76

Psychological critiques: Sigmund Freud

Revised

Austrian neurologist Sigmund Freud (1856–1939) argued that religion is an illusion:

- God has no reality, but is a creation of the human mind.
- The origins of religious belief lay with primitive tribes – the 'primal horde'.
- It leads to the **Oedipus complex**.
  - ○ The tension between the dominant male and the subordinate males (sons) culminates in the overthrow of the father.
  - ○ The guilt of the sons leads them to worship him.
  - ○ The **superego** then takes the place of the father as a source of authority.
- It represses antisocial impulses by inducing fear and guilt.
- God is a father substitute.
- Humanity is dependent upon religion to 'make his helplessness tolerable'.
- While humanity depends on this illusion, people will never be truly happy.

> **Oedipus complex** – the desire to possess one's mother and kill one's father, as theorised by Freud.
>
> **Superego** – the source of authority within a person.

Criticisms

- Freud assumed that all aspects of belief in God were immature, and he neglected the development of religious beliefs.
- Freud exaggerated the connection between belief in God and the psychopathological tendencies of religious belief. Freud's anti-religious stance may be thought just as neurotic as the religious preoccupations of others.
- Freud's approach has been criticised by scholars because Freud's methods allowed his biases to influence his data.

> **Key quote**
>
> 'Most post-Freudians think that his need to explain everything by sex tells us more about his obsessional neurosis than ours.'
>
> (Peter Moore)

> **Exam tip**
>
> Use Freud cautiously in your answers because Freud's influence in psychology has declined over the years, and his theories of the primal horde have been rejected by most scholars as mere guesswork.

> **Now test yourself**
>
> Tested
>
> 8 What did Freud think religion was?
>
> **Answer on page 76**

Carl Jung

Revised

Swiss psychologist Carl Jung (1875–1961) was concerned with the interplay between conscious and unconscious forces:

- He proposed two kinds of unconscious:
  - ○ Personal unconscious (shadow) includes those things about ourselves that we would like to forget.
  - ○ The **collective unconscious** refers to events that we all share, by virtue of having a common humanity.
- Jung maintained that religion was essential for a balanced psyche because it integrated the personality.

Criticisms

- Jung's view of empirical evidence and data is too broad.
- Not all of his research follows strict enough methods of verifying empirical evidence.

Exam practice answer guidance at **www.therevisionbutton.co.uk/myrevisionnotes**

Popularist critiques: Richard Dawkins

Revised

Evolutionary biologist Richard Dawkins argues that religious belief is dangerous, out of date and ridiculous. In the Channel 4 documentary *Tsunami: Where was God?* (December 2005), he claimed: 'I want people to stop believing'.

Dawkins' objections to religious belief are:

- A Darwinian world view makes belief in God unnecessary.
- The fact that humans exist at all is a remarkable enough coincidence of biology without looking for any greater significance.
- Evolution is the explanation for all living things.

- Claims of faith which lack any basis in empirical facts. They are supernatural explanations of the world which prevent humanity from investigating further.
- Religion offers an impoverished world view: 'The universe presented by organised religion is a poky little mediaeval universe' (*The Third Culture*, 1996).

Dawkins argues that religion leads to evil, and is like a virus that infects human minds. He uses the beliefs and practices of fundamentalist Islam and evangelical Christianity as examples to show:

- misleading education
- prejudice and ignorance
- a form of child abuse when referring to the children of Christian or Muslim parents as a 'Christian child' or a 'Muslim child'
- religiously motivated terrorism.

Criticisms

Dawkins explains his belief by reference to **memes** – ideas or beliefs which are analogous to genes. Memes spread rapidly from one person to another. But:

- If religious belief is a meme, passed through infection from one to another, so too is Dawkins' atheism.
- Dawkins' memes may well be bliks – ways of looking at the world that cannot be verified or falsified whatever evidence is presented.
- Melvin Tinker argues that 'Dawkins exhibits all the hallmarks of those forms of religion he so despises: vehemence, narrow-mindedness and intolerance. He is a "Fundamentalist" of the scientific kind' ('Dawkins' Dilemmas', *The Briefing*, Issue 337, October 2006).
- Dawkins reduces everything to scientific terms and argues that our only reason for living is to pass on DNA. Is this really the sole purpose of life?

- Can science explain everything?
- Is atheism scientifically proven?
- Dawkins claims that religion is harmful, but offers only simplified evidence. Melvin Tinkler said: 'He makes a value judgement that extremism and terror are "bad" things, but bad for whom?'
- A N Wilson describes Dawkins as: '... an arch simplifier, a hurler of unnecessary insults'.
- A N Wilson said: 'Why in God's name, do we take this silly, shallow scientist seriously?' (*Daily Mail*, 9 March).

> **Typical mistake**
>
> Be careful – Dawkins' views are very popular with candidates and some get carried away by them. Make sure that you don't just write about Dawkins, but use a range of scholars in your answer.

> **Now test yourself**
>
> Tested
>
> 9   What does Dawkins mean when he says that religion leads to evil?
> 10   What does Dawkins describe as a 'meme'?
>
> **Answers on page 76**

Other arguments for the non-existence of God

The problem of evil and suffering

The problem of evil challenges those who uphold the notion of an all-loving, all-powerful God. The dilemma is:

- If God is omnipotent (all-powerful), he can do anything. This means he could create a world that is free from evil and suffering and he could stop all evil and suffering.
- If God is omniscient and knows everything in the universe, he must know how to stop evil and suffering.
- If God is omnibenevolent (all-loving), he would wish to end all evil and suffering. No all-loving God would wish his creation to suffer for no reason.
- Yet evil and suffering do exist, so either God is not omnipotent or omnibenevolent *or* he does not exist.

Religious believers, however, argue:

- Suffering may be a test given to humanity by God to enable us to develop and mature.
- God gave humanity free will and therefore cannot interfere in human actions.

Key quotes

'Either God cannot abolish evil or he will not: if he cannot then he is not all-powerful, if he will not, then he is not all good'

(St Augustine)

'But the name of God means that he is infinite goodness. If, therefore, God existed, there would be no evil discoverable; but there is evil in the world. Therefore God does not exist'.

(Thomas Aquinas)

Science

Is it possible to explain the world religiously and non-religiously? Science has begun to explain the world and the universe in a non-religious way, highlighting that it is no longer possible to prove that God exists purely by looking at the workings of nature. Richard Dawkins argues that Darwin and others have shown that life on earth could have evolved rather than been created and he claims that the sole purpose of life is to pass on DNA – there is no need for God. At the Royal Institute Christmas Lecture in 1991 he observed: 'growing up in the universe … also means growing out of parochial and supernatural views of the universe.'

However, critics have argued against this view, claiming:

- The scientific evidence for evolution is limited.
- Passing on DNA is not the sole purpose of life. What about knowledge, discovery and moral development, for instance?

Key quotes

'Faith is the great cop-out, the great excuse to evade the need to think and evaluate the evidence.'

(Richard Dawkins)

'Dawkins exhibits all the hallmarks of those forms of religion he so despises; vehemence, narrow-mindedness and intolerance … he is a fundamentalist of the scientific kind.'

(Melvin Tinker)

The moral case against the existence of God

Revised

Why does God help some people and not others? Peter Vardy in *The Puzzle of God* (1999) questions the existence of an all-loving and powerful God on moral grounds: 'A God who intervenes at Lourdes to cure an old man of cancer but does not act to save starving millions in Ethiopia – such a God needs, at least, to face some hard moral questioning.' This leads to the moral criticism that God's actions seem to be incompatible with the notion of the love and justice of God. God appears to help some people, but not others. If he is indeed all loving and just, he should treat everyone equally.

On the other hand, God's actions in the Bible are clearly selective, and may suggest a broader purpose lies behind them, as Jesus claimed: 'Believe me when I say that I am in the Father and the Father is in me; or at least believe on the evidence of the miracles themselves' (John 14:11).

Key quote

'It seems strange that no miraculous intervention prevented Auschwitz or Hiroshima. The purposes apparently forwarded for some of the miracles acclaimed in the Christian tradition seem trivial by comparison.'

(Maurice Wiles)

Ockham's razor

Revised

Ockham's razor (from William of Ockham (1285–1349)), is the principle that in trying to understand something, the simplest explanation is usually the best. It may, therefore, be that God is, ultimately, the simplest explanation. The principle was used by Ockham to argue against attempts to justify the existence of God by reason alone, and he declared that the matter of God's existence could never be known only by faith, not proof.

Scriptural criticism and analysis

Revised

Scriptural criticism and analysis have discouraged a literal interpretation of the sacred text and shown that the writers may have been influenced by their social and cultural background at the time. Modern thinking suggests that the literal use of religious terms such as heaven, hell, demons and angels may be outdated mythical concepts. If this is the case, then the words of the Bible cannot prove the existence of God.

However, religious believers would argue that the scriptures are the inspired word of God and must be taken seriously.

Exam tip

Most candidates regard the problem of evil and suffering as the strongest atheistic argument. If you choose to take this approach in your exam, you must make sure that you do not spend time unnecessarily going over the solutions (free will, etc.). Instead, concentrate on the reasons why it is such a powerful argument against the existence of God.

Now test yourself

Tested

11 What is the principle of Ockham's razor?

Answer on page 76

Conclusion: is there a right answer?

The universe is religiously ambiguous, but does not explain itself. Some have argued that we can never know the answer, while others believe science may provide the answer. If it is not possible to decisively prove or disprove the existence of God, it is questionable whether the atheist has any stronger grounds than the theist. Perhaps a transcendent God is ultimately unknowable. As Bertrand Russell said in his famous 1948 radio debate: 'I can only say that you are looking for something which can't be got and which one ought not to expect to get.'

Exam practice

Answer the following as a test essay in 35 minutes.

(a) Examine two critiques of religious belief. **(18 marks)**

(b) Assess the view that atheism offers a more convincing answer than theism. **(12 marks)**

Answer guidance online

Online

Summary

✔ Atheism says that God does not exist.

✔ Agnosticism says it is not possible to be certain if God exists or not.

✔ Naturalism says that nothing exists except the natural universe.

✔ Scepticism says that there can be no certainty.

✔ Religion could be explained simply as functional – keeping society together (Durkheim).

✔ Religion may be the invention of the human mind (Marx).

✔ Religion may be an illusion (Freud).

✔ Religion lacks empirical evidence to support it (Dawkins).

2.1 Beliefs about life after death

Life after death

Our physical life will end someday but is there life after death (post-mortem existence) and if so, what is it like? There are several compelling reasons for believing that there is life after death:

- People are scared of death.
- It is hard to accept that this physical life is all that there is.
- Morality is only fulfilled when the good are rewarded (heaven) and the evil punished (hell).
- An afterlife would give enough time for human potential to be realised.
- If life is a holy and precious gift from God (the **sanctity of life**), then it should not end so quickly.
- Some religions hold **reincarnation** as a belief.

However, others say that there is no life after death because:

- Death is a biological function and a part of the natural process.
- The notion of life after death is meaningless and unnecessary.
- The empirical physical evidence of the end of the body at death makes it logically impossible to speak of an afterlife.
- To speak at all of a soul is a meaningless exercise, since it is impossible to verify its existence.
- The very phrase 'life after death' is an impossible contradiction since life and death are two mutually exclusive states.

> **Reincarnation** – the belief that the soul moves after death to another body, until it is finally released into a higher form.

> **Exam tip**
>
> The terms 'mind' and the 'soul' may be used in the examination to mean the same thing – the essential 'real person'. The soul is a more religious term. Both the words 'mind' and 'soul' refer to the thinking, feeling, willing and thoughtful consciousness and self-awareness of a person – what makes them a truly unique individual. You can readily use either or both words.

The relationship between the body and the mind/soul

Revised

What part of a person survives death and lives on? There are two viewpoints:

- **Monism**: the body and mind/soul are linked together to form one entity. Life after death therefore involves a body and mind/soul linked together.
- **Dualism**: the body and mind/soul are distinct and separate entities, though each can influence the other. Only the mind/soul lives on after death.

In the monistic view	In the dualistic view
• Human beings are psycho-physical unities. • A person is made up of the physical body and the mind, which determines mental behaviour. • There is no mind/soul that is distinct from the body and which survives death.	• Human beings have composite natures – partly material (physical body) and partly non-material (mind/soul). • The physical body and the mind/soul are regarded as distinct entities. • The mind/soul survives death.

This raises two key problems:

- If only the soul survives death, then a very important aspect of the human character is lost.
- If both body and soul are needed for eternal life, then how can the empirical evidence of physical death be explained?
- Philosopher Bertrand Russell (1872–1970) suggested that probably nothing survived: '… our mental life is bound up with brain structure and organised bodily energy. Therefore it is rational to suppose that mental life ceases when bodily life ceases' (*Russell on Religion*, 1999).

Now test yourself   Tested ☐

1 What is the monistic view of mind/soul and body?
2 What is the dualistic view of mind/soul and body?

Answers on page 76

Key quotes

'Man does not have a body, he is a body … he is flesh-animated-by-soul, the whole conceived as a psycho-physical unity.'

(J A T Robinson)

'Our soul is of a nature entirely dependent of the body and, consequently … is not bound to die with it and since we cannot see any other causes that destroy the soul, we are naturally led to conclude that it is immortal.'

(René Descartes)

Near-death experiences   Revised ☐

A near-death experience is said to occur when someone apparently dies (from all physical signs they appear to be dead), perhaps on the operating table, and is then resuscitated. Many who have experienced this, claim the following happened:

- They floated out of their bodies.
- They travelled down a tunnel and arrived in a place of light.
- They met either a dead relative, or a religious figure.
- They were given the choice to return to life.

In *The Light Beyond* (1984), psychologist Dr Raymond Moody (b. 1944) highlighted a number of problems:

- The experience could be a dream or hallucination.
- Feelings of peace may be due to drugs.
- It could be subconscious memories (**cryptomnesia**).
- Testimonies cannot be verified.

Moody felt that near-death experiences raised as many questions as answers: 'I am left, not with conclusions or evidence or proofs, but with something less definite – feelings, questions, analogies, puzzling facts to be explained.'

Typical mistake

A common mistake made by candidates is to treat a near-death experience as death. It is not, since the person is never truly dead in the first place. For instance, avoid writing 'the person dies and their soul leaves their body and goes to the gates of heaven' because this is not verifiable evidence, just a subjective interpretation of what may or may not have actually happened.

Now test yourself   Tested ☐

3 Describe a near-death experience.
4 Why is life after death a contradiction?
5 In what ways are human beings psycho-physical unities?

Answers on page 76

Reincarnation

Reincarnation, or **transmigration of the soul**, is the rebirth in another body (after physical death) of a person's personality or soul. It is claimed that reincarnated people:

- remember previous lives
- show physical marks similar to those they had in their previous life.

In Hinduism, life and death are regarded as part of the cycle of existence:

- On death, the soul is reborn again in another body.
- The soul receives a higher or lower rebirth depending on how the person lived their life.
- The good or bad actions a person does are called **karma**.
- This cycle goes on through many lives until the soul achieves ultimate reality (**nirvana**) and is united with Brahman.
- The soul itself is in a state of illusion, enclosed in a set of 'bodies':
  - the 'gross body' (**sthula sharira**), which is the physical body
  - the 'subtle body' (**linga sharira**), which is the mind, the intellect, the emotions and the spiritual aspect of a person.
- The aspects of a person that change in their lifetimes are called **samskaras**, or impressions.
- It is the subtle body that is reincarnated.
- The soul is not only reincarnated on earth.
- There are also other realms of existence where the soul has to face the consequences of the good or bad deeds (karma) done on earth.
- It is through repeated physical lives on earth that the soul ultimately discovers the path to perfection and enlightenment (**moksha**).

Key quote

'Just as a person casts off worn-out garments and puts on others that are new, even so does the disembodied soul cast off worn out bodies and takes on others that are new'

(*Bhagavad Gita*)

Exam tip

It is important to bear in mind that Hindu scholars have argued that there is empirical evidence of reincarnation. This evidence lies in the fact that reincarnation explains many strange occurrences in human life – for instance, our fear of death could stem from knowledge gained in previous lives.

Criticisms

If we accept that human personality is made up of a combination of the physical body, memory and psychological patterns (personal identity), then:

- On reincarnation, bodily continuity is lost.
- If we cannot remember our previous lives, then memory is lost too.
- This leaves only the psychological pattern of personal character.
- It would be impossible to know if one person is the reincarnation of another.
- The most it can offer is a vague memory linking all the past lives together.

Rebirth

Rebirth is a Buddhist concept that has certain similarities to the Hindu notion of reincarnation. It is based on the doctrine of anatta (no soul). The Buddha taught that everything is temporary and impermanent (anicca) and that all existence is imperfect and vulnerable to evil (dukkha).

Buddhism teaches that:

- A person is made up of the physical body and four mental elements: feeling, perception, moral will and consciousness, which are together called the nama-rupa (name form).

- When the physical body dies, the nama-rupa is released and the character aspects of the dead person are reborn into the new person.

- That rebirth is governed by karma – how good or bad a person has been in their previous life.

- The physical body is temporary; the real self is eternal and unchanging.

- Therefore, the soul must rid itself of all change and achieve nirvana, which is the end of rebirth.

- It does this through the gradual realisation, through a number of lifetimes, of the nature of the ultimate reality.

- In his book *Death and Eternal Life* (1983) John Hick describes rebirth: '… there is no ordinary-language self, but that the mind or self or person is a wholly temporal reality… there is no empirical self or person.'

Criticisms

There are criticisms of the concept of rebirth:

- It cannot be verified.

- It is difficult to assess if memory is retained from rebirth to rebirth.

- The Buddha taught the rebirths may not be on earth and even if they are, they need not be as human beings. In *The Book of Gradual Sayings*, he declared: '… more numerous are those beings who, deceasing as men, are reborn in **purgatory**, who are reborn in the wombs of animals, who are reborn in the Realm of Ghosts.'

- It is impossible to tell whether or not rebirth constitutes life after death in the accepted sense, for so much of it lies outside the earthly sphere of understanding.

- Hick observes in *Death and Eternal Life*: 'It may be that certain psychic formations which were part of the previous individual are now part of him. But if they are not accompanied by memory, can they be said to constitute the same person?'

> **Purgatory** – a place where lapsed believers go to be punished and then purified from sin.

Exam practice answer guidance at **www.therevisionbutton.co.uk/myrevisionnotes**

Bodily resurrection

Revised

Bodily resurrection is an important doctrine of Christianity. It is based on the notion that:

- At some future date (Judgement Day), God, as an act of love, will raise the dead to eternal life in bodily form.
- The re-creation by God of the individual is in physical form, but made of spirit, which can never die.
- Christ said: 'I am the resurrection and the life. He who believes in me, though he die, yet shall he live' (John 11:25).
- When Christ was resurrected, he had bodily form.
- The resurrected person is not the same as the one who died.
- The individual will have a spiritual body (**soma pneumatikon**), which contains all of their memories and characteristics and which will live forever.
- 'For the trumpet will sound, the dead will be raised imperishable, and we shall be changed' (1 Corinthians 15:52).

> **Typical mistake**
>
> There are always a number of candidates who write about bodily resurrection with no reference to Jesus Christ. The accounts of his resurrection are crucial to any answer so don't be afraid to refer to the Bible.

> **Now test yourself**
>
> Tested
>
> 6 What is reincarnation?
> 7 What is the resurrection of the body?
>
> **Answers on page 76**

Criticisms

There are criticisms of the concept of bodily resurrection:

- Is the resurrected body really 'us' or simply a copy of us?
- If we have truly died, then we cannot be brought back to life.
- Is the body resurrected in perfect health, with physical defects and illnesses cured?

Philosopher John Hick (1922–2012) attempted to answer this with his **replica theory**. He suggested that:

- If someone died and appeared in another place with the same memories and physical features then it would be right to regard this replica as the same person.
- An all-powerful God would be able to create a replica of a dead person, complete with all the individual's memories and characteristics.
- God could then create a world inhabited by resurrected persons.
- In *Philosophy of Religion* (1976), Hick said that life after death could be: '… as a resurrection replica in a different world altogether, a resurrection world inhabited only by resurrected persons.'

There are problems with this theory:

- God could make multiple replicas, which would undermine personal identity.
- A replica is not as valuable as the original.
- A replica is, by definition, not the same as the original.
- If bodily resurrection does not take place until the end of time, then how can life after death be verified now?

Hick offered the principle of **eschatological verification** – that one day, at the end of time, if there is life after death, we will know.

Immortality of the soul

In this view, the physical body will die, but the soul, which is the real self, cannot die because it is spiritual. In *Range of Reason* (1953), French philosopher Maritain (1882–1973) said:

> **A spiritual soul cannot be corrupted, since it possesses no physical matter ... the human soul cannot die. Once it exists, it cannot disappear; it will necessarily exist for ever.**

In *Phaedo*, Plato said that:

- The body belongs to the physical world and will one day cease to exist.

- The soul belongs to a higher realm and will endure for ever.

- The soul seeks to free itself from the physical world and go to the higher realm of true reality (the realm of the Forms), where it will be able to spend eternity contemplating truth, beauty and goodness.

- The physical body is made up of bits of the material world.

- The soul is made up of an invisible, intellectual and immaterial (non-physical) reality.

- The soul existed before birth and will continue to exist after the death of the body.

German philosopher Kant argued that:

- The purpose of existence is to achieve the **summum bonum** or complete good.

- Human beings cannot achieve this in one lifetime.

- God is morally obliged to help humanity to achieve the complete good by granting eternal life.

Where does the soul go? Heaven and hell

The traditional Christian view is that:

- If a dying person has received God's forgiveness for their wrong-doing, then they are said to die in a 'state of grace' and will go to heaven.

- Those who do not die in such a state will go either to hell, a place of eternal punishment, where the worst sinners go, or to purgatory, a place where lapsed believers go to be punished and then purified from sin.

In *The God Delusion* (2006), evolutionary biologist Richard Dawkins described purgatory as:

> **... a Hadean waiting room where dead souls go if their sins aren't bad enough to send them to Hell.**

John Hick regards the notion of Hell as:

> **... horrible and disturbing beyond words; and the thought of such torment being deliberately inflicted by divine decree is totally incompatible with the idea of God as infinite love.**

> *(Death and Eternal Life)*

> **Key quote**
>
> 'The *summum bonum* is only possible on the presupposition of the immortality of the soul.'
>
> (Immanuel Kant)

Aquinas regarded heaven as a beatific vision, which is a state of highest joy – the unchanging vision of God:

> ... we must not, therefore, imagine God in the beatific vision as some outside object to look at, but as dwelling within the very essence of our soul ...
>
> *(Summa Theologica)*

There are plenty of images of heaven in the Bible:

> I saw the Lord seated on the throne, high and exalted, and the train of his robe filled the temple. Above him were seraphs ... calling to one another: 'Holy, holy, holy is the Lord Almighty.'
>
> (Isaiah 6: 2–3)

Criticisms

There are criticisms of the concept of the immortality of the soul:

- How does the soul, without a physical body, relate to its surroundings and to other souls?
- Would this really be life after death?
- The individual will continue to exist, but will not have proper interaction with other people.

Now test yourself

8 Who proposed the replica theory?

9 What is eschatological verification?

10 Who called purgatory 'a Hadean waiting room'?

Answers on page 76

Tested

Conclusion: is there life after death?

It is questionable whether it is possible to speak meaningfully about life after death, since life and death are mutually exclusive. None of the views on life after death are completely convincing, mainly due to the lack of empirical evidence. Some people are convinced that the concept of life after death is just a kind of social control to encourage good behaviour and satisfaction in this life. Others feel that life after death is just a comforting idea for those who fear death. Perhaps the answer lies in thinking of life after death as anti-realist, rather than thinking of it as a real mode of being.

Key quote

'If the human potential is to be fulfilled in the lives of individuals, these lives must be prolonged far beyond the limits of our present bodily existence.'

(John Hick)

Exam practice

Answer the following as a test essay in 35 minutes.

(a) Examine the concepts of the immortality of the soul with the resurrection of the body. **(18 marks)**

(b) To what extent is one of these a more convincing argument for life after death than the other? **(12 marks)**

Answer guidance online

Online

Summary

- ✔ Monism – body and mind are linked.
- ✔ Dualism – body and mind are not necessarily linked.
- ✔ Limited scientific evidence concerning life after death – best example is near-death experiences.
- ✔ Several possibilities for life after death – immortality of soul, reincarnation, rebirth, bodily resurrection.
- ✔ Life after death is necessary to achieve 'summum bonum' (Kant).
- ✔ We will only know the truth at the end of time – eschatological verification (Hick).
- ✔ Bible suggests bodily resurrection – Christ as example.
- ✔ No empirical evidence as to nature of life after death.
- ✔ What survives – mind? Soul? And is it really us?
- ✔ Is life after death a meaningful concept anyway? (Flew).

2.2 Religious language

Key concepts

Religious language is about the way we speak about God and religious belief. It includes:

- descriptions of the nature of God, such as 'omniscient'
- descriptions of religious belief, such as 'heaven'
- religious technical terms, such as 'sin'
- ordinary words that have a special religious meaning, such as 'love'.

The main problems with religious language are:

- It is difficult to use human words to describe a transcendent God who is above and beyond all human experience.
- Human words are inadequate and this causes misunderstandings.
- Some believe that it is impossible to speak meaningfully about God.

Religious language and meaning:

- 'Meaning' is what a statement says.
- 'Meaningful' means that it makes sense.
- Language can be both true and meaningful.
- A statement is meaningful if it makes sense to us – even if we don't agree with it.
- 'Today is Monday' makes sense, even on a Tuesday.
- This makes sense because we can verify it.
- Religious statements have meaning, but may not be meaningful.
- This is because religious statements may not be verifiable.

> **Key quote**
>
> 'To say that God exists is to make a metaphysical utterance which cannot be either true or false. And by the same criterion, no sentence which purports to describe the nature of a transcendent God can possess any literal significance.'
>
> (A J Ayer)

The function of language is to communicate clearly with others. In *Closing Statutes and Poetics* (1960), linguist Roman Jakobson (1896–1982) noted six functions of language:

- referential – describing situations or things ('The leaves are falling')
- expressive – describing feelings or emotions ('Wow! Look at that!')
- conative – a command or request ('Come here!')
- poetic – a poem or saying/slogan ('Easy come, easy go')
- phatic – greetings or casual conversations ('Hi. Nice weather we're having')
- **metalingual** – talking about yourself ('I feel fine').

Religious statements may fit some or all of these.

> **Metalingual** – using a story or text to explain the meaning of something.

Religious language and realism/anti-realism

Realism, or realist language, deals with statements that can be proved to be either true or false. They can:

- contain empirically provable statements ('The sky is blue')
- be statements that have meaning for some people, such as religious believers ('God exists')
- be statements of command or desire ('Please go away!').

Anti-realist statements are those that should not be taken literally, but are understood in other ways, such as:

- symbols, metaphors, myths, moral commands
- statements that are true within a group, for instance religious sayings such as 'Jesus died for my sins'.

The truth or falsity of a statement depends on its context.

> **Key quote**
>
> Flew described realist language as '… crypto commands, expressions of wishes, disguised ejaculations, concealed ethics, or anything else but assertions.'
>
> (Anthony Flew)

> **Cognitive/Realist** – deals with what is true in the real world.

Cognitive and non-cognitive language

Some religious concepts can be described in human words when **cognitive (realist)** language is used, for example:

- factual statements that can be empirically proved to be either true or false ('St Paul's Cathedral is in London')
- statements that contain meaningful factual content for believers ('Jesus was born in Bethlehem').

There are other religious terms that, although not factually true, can be understood using non-cognitive (anti-realist) language, for example:

- symbolic statements ('The Cross is my salvation')
- mythical statements/stories (the story of Noah's Ark)
- oral commands ('Love your neighbour')
- statements that express a religious truth for believers ('Jesus is the Son of God').

> **Exam tip**
>
> Religious language questions are best answered by giving plenty of real-life examples. For instance, don't just say 'cognitive language' but add an example, such as 'all bachelors are male'.

> **Now test yourself**
>
> Tested
>
> 1 What is realist language?
> 2 What is a non-cognitive statement?
> 3 Why do some scholars say that statements about life after death are meaningless?
> 4 Why might statements about God be meaningless?
>
> Answers on page 76

The verification principle

Can religious terms that cannot be empirically tested be meaningful? In the 1920s a group of philosophers known as the Vienna Circle developed the **verification principle**. They suggested that language is meaningful if it can be defined in terms of the real world. To be meaningful, a statement must be one of the following:

- analytic – true by definition ('a bachelor is unmarried')
- mathematical – true by the rules of mathematics ('2+2=4', even if we don't have two of anything in particular)
- synthetic – true or false by empirical testing ('all swans are white').

The Vienna Circle said that religious statements were meaningless since they did not satisfy any of these criteria. British philosopher A J Ayer, in *Language, Truth and Logic,* went further. He claimed that:

- The existence of God could not be rationally demonstrated.
- The term 'god' is a **metaphysical** term referring to a transcendent being that could not be proved.
- Any statement about God was therefore meaningless.
- Descriptions of the soul, life after death and heaven were also meaningless because they could not be verified.
- The testimony of those who said they had undergone a religious experience could not be empirically verified and were also meaningless.

> **Metaphysical** – beyond or outside the laws of science.

Criticisms

However, the verification principle has problems because many of the statements it claims are meaningless do have meaning, for example:

- Statements that express opinions or emotions have meaning.
- Ethical and moral statements are not empirically verifiable, but certainly have meaning.
- Laws of science have meaning but cannot be always be completely verified. For example, we do not know if gravity always works in the same way and will continue to do so in the future. It may end tomorrow!
- Historical statements are meaningful even when there is no one alive who could claim to have experienced the events.
- The verification principle cannot itself be verified.

In response, Ayer suggested a strong and weak form of the verification principle:

- Strong verification occurs when there is no doubt that a statement is true ('The moon orbits the earth').
- Weak verification occurs where there is not absolute certainty, but where there is a strong likelihood of truth ('Henry V won the Battle of Agincourt').

Key quote

'A proposition is verifiable in the strong sense if, and only if, its truth can be conclusively established … but it is verifiable in the weak sense if it is possible for experience to render it probable.'

(A J Ayer)

Typical mistake

Don't just accept the verification principle on face value. Remember that it has weaknesses as well and recent scholars have begun to argue differently. Theologian Keith Ward (b. 1938) in *Holding Fast to God* (1994) observed that God's existence could be verified in principle since: 'If I were God I would be able to check the truth of my own existence.'

Now test yourself   Tested ☐

5   What is cognitive language?
6   What is a myth?
7   What is a synthetic statement?
8   Define strong and weak verification and give an example of each.

Answers on page 76

The falsification principle

The **falsification principle** is almost the reverse of the verification principle in that it asks what would be needed to prove a religious language statement to be false. John Hick in *Faith and Knowledge* (1989) said:

> In order to say something which may possibly be true, we must say something which may possibly be false.

In support of the falsification principle, philosopher Anthony Flew took the scientific view that:

- to check the truth of something means to check the falseness of it as well
- 'What would have to occur or to have occurred to constitute for you a disproof of the love of, or the existence of, God?'
- religious believers often do not allow evidence against the existence of God and instead hide behind vague answers, such as 'God's love is a mystery' when they cannot explain things, such as why God seems to allow terrible things to happen.
- religious language was meaningless because believers did not allow for any of their beliefs about God to be proved false.

Criticisms

Moral philosopher R M Hare criticised the falsification principle by claiming that:

- When believers use religious language, they are using it in a special way.
- This is a blik – a unique way of seeing the world, which cannot be proved to be true or false.
- Religious believers use religious language to express beliefs that are important to them and which make a difference to their lives that can be empirically observed.
- Religious language can be meaningful because it expresses an intention to follow a certain code of conduct.

The via negativa

The **via negativa** is the view that:

- The truth about God can be discovered by speaking negatively about Him – the way to find out what God is like is first to discover what He is not like.
- This is the **principle of negation**.
- When using human language to describe the qualities of God, it is easier to say what He is not.

Criticisms

There are criticisms of the via negativa:

- It does not allow God to be described in factual terms.
- To say that God can only be spoken of in negatives means denying the existence of God altogether.
- Believers always want to speak positively about God.

Now test yourself

9   What is the via negativa?

Answer on page 76

Different types of religious language

In religious language, some words are not to be taken literally and the meaning of words and phrases can often depend on an understanding of the way religious language is used. There are several different ways in which such language is used.

Univocal language

- Using words and phrases in their everyday sense, for example, using 'God's love' and 'John's love' to mean the same thing.
- In this way it is possible to understand God because we know the nature of God's love because we understand human love.
- But univocal language does not always work because if we refer to God and people in the same way, then we are unable to tell the difference between them.

Equivocal language

- Using the same words but in a totally different way.
- The nature of God is so different from the nature of humanity that when we refer to God as being 'loving' we are using the word in a different way.
- God's love is not of the same nature as human love.
- Using equivocal language simply highlights how God's qualities are similar, yet distinct, from human ones.

Analogical language

- Using human words such as 'love' and applying them in a similar but not identical way to God.
- God's love is similar to human love but superior.
- Analogy allows people to speak meaningfully about God, by using human terms to describe, in a relative way, the qualities of God.
- Aquinas called this the 'gradation to be found in things'.
- All the love in humanity came first from God and, therefore, God and humanity are 'analogously related'.
- All the positive qualities of humanity belong to God in a greater way.

There are two types of analogy:

- **Analogy of proportionality** – all good qualities belong infinitely to God and, in proportion, to humans.
- **Analogy of attribution** – God is the cause of all good things in humans and therefore God's attributes are at a higher level than our own. Human love is a pale reflection of God's love.

> **Exam tip**
>
> This is a popular area for questions. Make sure you know what all the technical terms mean and have some examples ready. Remember to include strengths and weaknesses in your answer, together with a range of scholarly opinions.

> **Typical mistake**
>
> Many students find this section complex and think that just using technical terms is sufficient. Be careful and make sure you back up what you say with evidence. In the exam, what you say must be 'supported substantially by evidence and reasoning'.

> **Exam tip**
>
> Don't forget that, to get a high grade in your examination, your answer must be 'expressed accurately and fluently and using a range of technical vocabulary.'

> **Now test yourself**
>
> Tested
>
> 10 What is univocal language?
>
> 11 Explain the meaning of the phrase 'analogy of proportionality'.
>
> **Answers on page 76**

Symbolic language

- A symbol is something that identifies the thing that it is referring to and participates in the meaning of that concept. For example, a flag is a symbol of national unity.
- Symbols can be words, pictures, objects and actions.
- In most religious traditions symbols are very important.
- The cross in Christianity identifies the religion and participates in the Christian concept of the death and resurrection of Jesus (the crucifix).
- Symbols go beyond factual information and should not be interpreted literally.
- The most common types of symbolic language are myths and metaphors.

Symbolism and myth

Revised

Symbols are important in religious language because they are a very subtle mode of communication which goes beyond mere facts. They are non-cognitive and go beyond normal understanding. They are, according to philosopher Paul Tillich in *Systematic Theology* (1951), a positive way of expressing the nature of God in a way that people can easily understand.

The most common kinds of symbolic language found in religion are in the form of myths. A myth is a story that uses symbols to express a truth when it is not known for certain what actually happened. Several Bible stories are not literally true, but carry a symbolic meaning. For example:

- the virgin birth – not necessarily literally true, but a symbolic story that reflects the purity of Christ's birth and origin
- Jonah and the whale – a story that symbolises Jonah's feeling of being trapped and forgotten by God
- the story of Job – the symbolic story of how a man retained his faith in God despite great hardship
- Noah's Ark – probably a myth highlighting the sinful nature of humanity and the love of God for those who are righteous
- the nativity story – probably a myth depicting the birth of Jesus as a significant religious event.

Criticisms

The main problems with the use of symbolism in religious language:

- It is difficult to know exactly what the symbols mean and so the original meaning may be lost.
- Symbolic objects may become the focus of worship.
- Symbols and myths become outdated.

German theologian Rudolph Bultmann (1884–1976) argued that:

- In order to find out the truth of God, religious language should be demythologised.
- All the myths contained in the scriptures should be removed.
- The real truth of the scriptures would then be revealed.
- This would help the faith of religious believers.

Language games

In *Philosophical Investigations* (1936), philosopher Ludwig Wittgenstein (1889–1958) suggested a postmodern approach to language:

- All language is a game and in every 'form of life' words are used within the context of the subject area or 'game'.

- All 'forms of life' have their own language and have their own rules concerning meaning – medical language is understood by doctors, but not by bakers.

- The language in the game is not about making true statements for everyone, but about communicating meaning to other people in the same game.

- Religious language is therefore meaningful for those in the religious language game.

- These statements do not have to be meaningful to anyone else outside the game.

- Each game has its own 'criteria of coherence', which can only be understood by playing the right game by the right rules.

Key quote

'I think differently, in a different way. I say different things to myself. I have a different picture.'

(Ludwig Wittgenstein)

Strengths and weaknesses

Strengths	Weaknesses
• Believers can learn the rules of religious language. • Religious language games defend religion against criticisms from other 'forms of life' because truth depends on which 'game' a person is in.	• Religious language games do not allow for truth claims to be empirically tested. • Religious language is only for those inside the game. • The rules of the games cannot be changed to allow outsiders in.

Conclusion: does religious language have any value?

Religious language is the way people speak about God, what they believe and why they believe it. It is about worship, dogma, doctrine and ideas. Yet no theory of religious language satisfies everyone. Religious language is very complex because it encompasses so many ideas and beliefs and, although it offers no empirical truths, it can offer significant insights into the nature of human belief in God. It neither proves nor disproves whether God exists, but it expresses belief and faith in something beyond the human world. In *Philosophy and the Christian Faith* (1968), philosopher Colin Brown wryly observed: 'Divine truth has to be refracted and expressed in terms of human words and finite images.'

Exam practice

Answer the following as a test essay in 35 minutes.

(a) Examine the view that all religious language claims are meaningless because they cannot be verified. **(18 marks)**

(b) Discuss the extent to which language games solve the problem of religious language. **(12 marks)**

Answer guidance online

Online

Summary

✔ Religious language is used to speak about God and religious belief.

✔ The main problem is that human language is often inadequate when speaking about God.

✔ Some religious language statements are literal and can be proved to be true or false (realist).

✔ Some religious language statements are not literally true but may be understood in other ways e.g. analogy (anti-realist).

✔ Some scholars have argued that religious language is meaningless because it cannot be verified.

✔ Others argue that it can be understood in symbolic, analogous or univocal ways.

✔ Others highlight the importance of myth in religious language, particularly in relation to scripture.

✔ Some see religious language as part of a 'language game', in that it only has meaning in a particular context which is unique to it ('form of life').

3.1 Critiques of the relationship between religion and morality

Key concepts

The relationship between religion and morality is a difficult one, raising many complex questions:

- Is it possible to be religious but not moral?
- Is it possible to be moral but not religious?
- What is the relationship between God and goodness?
- Is there a supreme moral lawgiver?
- If God does not exist, then is everything permissible?
- How can we know if religious morality really does reflect God's will?

Key quote

'Many **religionists** maintain that morality is a gift from a supernatural deity and that, to be moral, we must obey the supposed demands of that deity …. Non-believers, by contrast, recognize that morality is based on human needs. Thus, morality is designed to benefit humans rather than to serve an imaginary god.'

(Jon Nelson)

Religionist – one who supports the religious standpoint.

Morality and the existence of God

St Thomas Aquinas ─────────────────────────── Revised ☐

In the *Summa Theologica*, philosopher and theologian St Thomas Aquinas argued that the gradation to be found in things pointed irrefutably to the existence of God:

> Among beings there are some more and some less good, true, noble and the like ... so that there is something which is truest, something best, something noblest ... Therefore there must also be something which is to all beings the cause of their being, goodness, and every other perfection, and this we call God.

Aquinas's arguments were based on Plato's eternal forms, or archetypes, which suggested that:

- The human mind is aware of goodness, which is a pale copy of a greater, unseen reality, which is eternal.
- The goodness, virtue, or truth found in human beings and in the world is a reflection of the perfect goodness of God.
- God, being perfect in goodness, is also perfect in his existence.
- God's moral perfection is therefore evidence for his existence.

This view was supported by philosopher F C Copleston (1907–94), who claimed:

> I do think that all goodness reflects God in some way and proceeds from him, so that in a sense the man who loves what is truly good, loves God.
>
> (Cited in *The Existence of God*, ed John Hick, 1968)

However, while Copleston maintained that it was necessary to refer to God in order to be able to distinguish between good and evil, philosopher Bertrand Russell disagreed, saying:

> I love the things that I think are good, and I hate the things that I think are bad. I don't say that these things are good because they participate in the Divine goodness.
>
> (Cited in *The Existence of God*, ed John Hick, 1968)

Is there such a thing as religious morality?

Revised ☐

For many religious believers, obeying **religious moral commands** is important because they believe that they will be rewarded or punished by God in the hereafter. On the other hand, if there is no God to support the demands of religious moral commands, then there is no threat of punishment or promise of reward, and so morality is meaningless. In other words, if God does not exist, then everything is permitted.

Exam tip

Although you don't need to write about the moral argument in the exam, it is an important way in to understanding why links are made between God, religion and morality. The most convincing reason for why religious believers believe they should be moral is that God commands them to be so.

The Euthyphro dilemma

Revised ☐

Some people argue that obeying religious moral commands can lead to wrongful, or even dangerous, conclusions. This is best seen in Plato's famous **Euthyphro dilemma**.

Let's take the first position:

- Does God command X because it is good?
- In this case, goodness exists as something separate from God. God is the means by which humanity receives moral knowledge, but that knowledge has not come directly from God's moral nature. God cannot bring goodness into being. This is a very limited view of God.

And the second position:

- Is X good because God commands it?
- In this case, God is the direct source of moral knowledge. God's commands establish what is good, and nothing can be good unless God commands it. However, if this is the case, then the answer to the question 'Why is God good?' has to be 'Because he obeys his own commands', which seems a rather limited understanding of God's goodness. God makes the command as an omnipotent creator of moral standards and without Him there would be no moral right and wrong.

Religious moral commands – commands coming from God.

Euthyphro dilemma – Does God command X because it is good or is X good because God commands it?

Key quote

'Then tell me, what do you say the holy is? And what is the unholy? For consider, is the holy loved by the gods because it is holy? Or is it holy because it is loved by the gods?'

(Plato)

This raises a number of problems:

- Does God's commanding something to be done provide sufficient grounds to say that it is moral?
- This has the effect of making the moral law **arbitrary**, since it depends on God's random feelings.
- If God commanded someone to kill all homeless people, would that make it morally right to do so?
- According to the second position, it would be.
- But how would we know if we are correctly interpreting God's command?
- If we say no, because we know that God would not command such a thing, then we are saying that killing homeless people is wrong in itself.
- In which case, we don't need God to provide moral commandments and standards – we are able to make them for ourselves.

There are other difficult issues. In the case of the first position:

- How do we deal with situations in which God does not expressly give a command?
- Does it mean that anything that God commands becomes a moral law?
- Non-believers also act in a moral way – they get their moral standards without reference to God.
- How can we verify that the good are rewarded and the bad punished in the afterlife?

> **Arbitrary** – depending on random factors.

> **Typical mistake**
>
> Don't get drawn into the trap of writing too many ideas in list form. The exam criteria requires candidates to express themselves 'in a coherent and well-organised argument' – which means you should write in full sentences.

Now test yourself   Tested ☐

1   What is the Euthyphro dilemma?

Answer on page 76

In the case of the second position:

- If God simply commands that which is good, then where does morality originally come from?
- Does God operate according to moral laws already in place in the universe?
- If so, is God limited by laws of morality?
- Is he, therefore, God at all?

Philosopher Jean Porter in *Moral Action and Christian Ethics* (1995), observed:

> Yet there is something deeply disturbing about the argument that people ought to be prepared to accept suffering ... which could be alleviated ... for no other reason than that God has not given us the authority to act in the appropriate ways. Is the God of love so easily offended or is God's authority so precarious?

A dilemma: Abraham and Isaac

The more difficult of the two positions in the Euthyphro dilemma is the second one: if a moral command is good because God commands it, then does it really mean that *anything* God commanded would be good?

This is demonstrated in the biblical story of Abraham, a follower of God, when he is asked by God to kill his only son Isaac as a sacrificial offering:

> **After these things, God tested Abraham. He said to him, 'Abraham!' And he said, 'Here I am'. He said, 'Take your son, your only son, Isaac, whom you love, and go to the land of Moriah, and offer him as a burnt offering on one of the mountains that I shall show you.'**
>
> (Genesis 22:1–2)

Abraham is a man of faith and takes Isaac to be sacrificed. It is only after he has raised his knife to strike Isaac that God intervenes and saves the boy. Abraham's willingness to kill Isaac has been enough for God to know that he would not withhold his only son from him. A ram is found in a thicket and offered in Isaac's place.

Did God command what is good here? Danish philosopher Søren Kierkegaard (1813–55) questioned if it was ever reasonable for someone to be asked to disregard what he believes to be right and instead follow the demands of his religious faith. Kierkegaard reached the conclusion that it was, since faith (in God) is the most important thing. Doing the will of God goes beyond human understanding of morality and being bound to the human moral law of society would be a hindrance to fulfilling God's will.

In *Varities of Unbelief* (2000) John Habgood observes that Abraham's situation is resolved by a new encounter with God. God's right to put Abraham under such severe conditions of testing is justified by his subsequent graciousness: 'The fact that God answered at all, even though he said nothing new, was what made the difference.'

Others disagree – philosopher Anthony Flew believed that God's actions in this incident bring up serious moral questions. Flew asked 'just what would have to happen not merely (morally and wrongly) to tempt but also (logically and rightly) to entitle us to say "God does not love us" or even "God does not exist"?' (*Theology and Falsification*, 1950).

> **Key quote**
>
> 'The God of the Old Testament is arguably the most unpleasant character in all fiction: jealous and proud of it; a petty, unjust, unforgiving control-freak; a vindictive, bloodthirsty ethnic cleanser; a misogynistic, homophobic, racist, infanticidal, genocidal, filicidal, pestilential, megalomaniacal, sadomasochistic, capriciously malevolent bully.'
>
> (Richard Dawkins)

> **Now test yourself**
>
> 2 Who said that we are entitled to say 'God does not love us'?
>
> **Answer on page 76**
>
> Tested

How reliable is religious moral teaching?

Those who do not believe in the authority of sacred texts argue that such moral teaching may be unreliable because:

- Sacred texts are culturally relative and belong to a particular time period.
- If religious believers are morally good only in the hope of receiving divine reward and avoiding punishment, is this genuine goodness?
- Too much pressure is put on religious believers to live up to unrealistic standards of goodness.
- The demands of religious morality are irrelevant today.

- Society only appeals to religious morality in times of crisis, not for guidance on daily moral living.
- Religious morality is outdated and can prevent moral and scientific progress.

Examples of religious morality which have caused concern to some include:

- condemnation of certain medical services (such as abortion) or medical research topics (such as embryonic stem cells)
- condemnation of certain types of sexual behaviour (such as homosexuality)
- discrimination against women.

A real-life example of **an absolutist approach to deriving morality from religion** is shown in the teachings and actions of some extreme religious groups, for instance the Westboro Baptist Church, which campaigns against homosexuality and against American society as a whole for supporting homosexuality. The members of this church base their campaign on an literal and absolutist interpretation of the words in Leviticus 18:22 which state: 'Do not lie with a man as with a woman … that is detestable.' Taking these words as the literal truth, the church members refuse to consider the later teachings of Jesus to 'love your neighbour as yourself' (Mark 12:31). As a result, they can see no reconciliation or moral compromise between the church and the homosexual community.

An example of **conflicting moralities** can be seen in the different stands taken by the Catholic and the Protestant Churches on the moral issue of divorce. The source of the conflict is the words of Jesus. In Mark 10:11, Jesus says: 'Anyone who divorces his wife and marries another woman commits adultery with her.' The Catholic Church interprets this to mean that there can be no divorce for Catholics. On the other hand, in Matthew 19:9, the words of Jesus are recorded as: 'Anyone who divorces his wife, except for marital unfaithfulness, and marries another woman commits adultery with her.' For Protestants, this means that there can be divorce for marital unfaithfulness. There is a serious conflict of morality over the interpretation of a few words.

> **Exam tip**
>
> Using examples in your answer can be very helpful in explaining the meaning of difficult concepts. They help you to fulfil the exam criteria of having 'examples appropriately deployed to show a clear understanding of the main issues.'

> **Now test yourself**
> Tested ☐
>
> 3 What moral issue does the Westboro Baptist Church campaign against?
> 4 How does the teaching of Jesus differ in Matthew's gospel from that in Mark's gospel?
>
> **Answers on page 76**

Friedrich Nietzsche

Philosopher Friedrich Nietzsche (1844–1900) in his work *On the Genealogy of Morality* (1884), stated that there were two kinds of morality. The first, which he called **natural morality**, is the morality of strength, power and dominance. It covers such notions as courage, truthfulness, trust and self-worth. Those who have this morality are the masters, and have power and authority over others. They are, according to Nietzsche, the creators of morality.

In contrast, the second type of morality is **slave morality**, which is the morality of the poor and weak. It is the reverse of natural morality and values actions such as pity and compassion. It is a reaction to the oppression of the strong. It does not fight the strong, but tries to make them adopt weak values as well. Nietzsche used the biblical teachings of Jesus – who spoke of compassion, love, pity and forgiveness and said that religion tries to force these slave values on all – weak and strong, master and slave alike. Nietzsche believed that, in the West, slave morality had won, calling it 'the collective degeneration of man'. He hoped that, one day, both types of morality would join together to form a common morality for all.

> **Natural morality** – 'good' can be seen in what is natural.
>
> **Slave morality** – the morality of the poor and weak.

Richard Dawkins

Richard Dawkins, the evolutionary biologist claims that:

- Religion leads to evil, like a virus that infects human minds.
- Religious faith is: 'An indulgence of irrationality that is nourishing extremism, division and terror' (The Root of all Evil?, Channel 4, January 2006).
- Religion is responsible for misleading education, prejudice and ignorance.
- The events of 9/11 and 7/7 were the result of religiously motivated terrorism.

Dawkins argues that morality evolves from society. It is not given by God. To have morality is part of what it means to be a society.

However, philosopher A C Grayling (b. 1949) puts forward an argument for the irrelevance of religion to contemporary morality:

> **Key quote**
>
> 'Many of us saw religion as harmless nonsense … September 11th changed all that. Revealed faith is not harmless nonsense, it can be lethally dangerous nonsense … dangerous because we have all bought into a weird respect, which uniquely protects religion from normal criticism. Let's now stop being so damned respectful!'
>
> (Richard Dawkins)

> There is a widespread supposition that a religious ethic … has to be good for individuals and society because it is inherently more likely to make them good. This view is troubling because it is false: religion is precisely the wrong resource for thinking about moral issues in the contemporary world, and indeed subverts moral debate.
>
> (*What is Good?*, 2003)

> **Now test yourself** Tested
>
> 5 Who spoke about a 'slave morality'?
> 6 Why did Dawkins call religion a 'virus'?
> 7 Who claimed that religion subverts moral debate?
>
> **Answers on page 76**

Conclusion: should religious morality be only for religious believers?

Many modern scholars feel that religious morality should be left to religious believers, and that it is not for society as a whole. Philosopher R A Sharpe (1935–2006) in *The Moral Case Against Religious Belief* (1997), highlighted what he saw as the absurdity of the Roman Catholic prohibition on contraception: 'Is it remotely conceivable that God should be interested in whether people use a condom rather than the rhythm method of contraception?'

He is supported by American philosopher Stephen Weinberg (b. 1933), who writes in *A Designer Universe* (1999): 'Without religion you have good people doing good things, and evil people doing evil things. But for good people to do evil things, it takes religion.'

However, support for some kind of universal religious morality still exists. Habgood noticed how, when communist regimes in Russia and elsewhere collapsed, the people soon returned to religious morality: 'Even atheists, when faced with a crisis of confidence, may see the need for something more than instinct, custom and social convention.'

Now test yourself

Tested ☐

8 According to Habgood, what happened when the communist regime in Russia collapsed?

Answer on page 76

Exam practice

Answer the following as a test essay in 35 minutes.

(a) Explain one critique of the link between religion and morality. **(18 marks)**

(b) To what extent does it succeed in showing the fact that there is no link between religion and morality? **(12 marks)**

Answer guidance online

Online ☐

Summary

- Looks at the question of whether or not it is possible to be moral and not religious.
- Examines the relationship between God and goodness.
- Goodness in humans is a 'pale reflection' of the goodness of God (Aquinas).
- Euthyphro Dilemma – does God command X because it is good, or is X good because God commands it?
- The truth of religious morality depends upon an answer to the question 'Does God exist?'.
- Religious moral teachings may be out-dated and no longer applicable.
- Nietzsche thought that religion encouraged a 'slave morality'.
- Dawkins argues that religion leads to evil.
- No empirical evidence to support a link between religion and morality.

3.2 Deontology, natural moral law and virtue ethics

Deontology: key concepts

Deontological theories are based on the view that there are certain actions that are right or wrong in themselves, not in the consequences of the action. Actions are right or wrong simply because they are and without reference to the outcome.

There are several forms of **deontology**:

- **Rights**: An action is morally right if it respects the rights that all humans have, for example, do not murder.
- **Duty**: An action is morally right if it is in line with a set of agreed duties and obligations, for example, allowing free speech.
- **Contractualism**: An action is morally right if it is in agreement with the rules that govern a social relationship or contract, for example, drive on the right-hand side of the road.
- **Divine command ethics**: An action is morally right if it is in agreement with rules and duties established by God, for example, do not commit adultery.
- **Monistic deontology**: An action is morally right if it agrees with a single deontological principle which guides all other principles, for example, killing is wrong.

Deontologists must:

- perform actions that are good in themselves
- refrain from performing those actions that are known to be wrong
- not violate a rule or constraint even if serious harm will occur
- not favour one person over another
- not lie
- follow absolute standards against which questions of morality and moral decision-making can be judged.

These moral standards come from fundamental sources of morality, including human nature, reason, the universe and God. They remain unchanging.

> **Deontology** – certain moral actions are right or wrong in themselves.

> **Exam tip**
>
> Don't forget that deontological constraints tend to be formulated as negatives: 'do not' rather than 'do'. These tell people what is obligatory or duty. There are two strands – what is permissible and what is impermissible. For instance, 'you may drink alcohol in private, but not in public'.

> **Key quote**
>
> Jesus taught that there was more to goodness than doing good actions alone: 'If you love those who love you, what reward will you get? Are not even the tax collectors doing that? And if you greet only your brothers, what are you doing more than others? Do not even pagans do that? Be perfect, therefore, as your heavenly Father is perfect.'
>
> (Matthew 5:46–48)

The problem with deontology   Revised

- A deontologist is not required to consider the consequences of an act; they can say in advance whether an action is right or wrong.
- Intuition may be enough to identify the moral value of an action.
- However, methods of identifying whether actions are right and wrong can be flawed because unbreakable moral laws cannot be reliably identified unless we can also identify the law giver and a reliable means of settling disputes concerning them.
- It allows a person to act morally just by obeying rules.

> **Typical mistake**
>
> Don't forget that evaluation of an argument means more than just writing out lists of strengths and weaknesses. The assessment criteria require that you express a point of view accurately, fluently and supported by evidence.

Exam practice answer guidance at **www.therevisionbutton.co.uk/myrevisionnotes**

Immanuel Kant

Perhaps the most famous deontological view was that of German philosopher Immanuel Kant. Kant's moral theory was:

- The reason for performing any given action is that it is morally obligatory to do so.
- This is the only correct motivation for an action.
- Following the correct moral rules is not enough.
- We must also have the correct motivation.
- Right duties and obligations are determined objectively and absolutely.

- All people possess reason and a conscience.
- Therefore all people can arrive at an understanding of moral truths independent of experience.
- Morality is *a priori* because reason is universal and moral reasoning would lead to the same results over and over again.
- The acceptance of other guides to morality, such as **utilitarianism**, is always mistaken.

Kant argued that:

- The universe is essentially just.
- Moral law will be satisfied (the good rewarded and the bad punished) in a post-mortem existence.
- The existence of God is a necessary requirement of a just universe and for the moral law to be balanced.
- True morality should not depend on individual likes and dislikes or other external circumstances.
- Moral commands are **categorical imperatives** and ends in themselves.
- They express an absolute and unconditional duty to act in a certain way.
- They are of supreme importance.
- If we act according to our duty in any given circumstances we will act rightly.
- Duty is better than personal inclinations and unworthy motives.

> **Utilitarianism** – the value of something is determined by its usefulness.
>
> **Categorical imperative** – things that should be done without conditions attached.

Kant was convinced that the categorical imperative that provides the fundamental moral groundwork for all actions is the **principle of universalisability**. As set out in his *Formula of the Law of Nature* the principle of universalisability is:

- Human beings must 'act in such a way that their actions might become a universal law'.
- If the rule governing our actions cannot be universalised, then it is not morally acceptable.
- If you cannot enforce that everyone follow the same rule, then it is not a moral rule, for example, do not discriminate.

> **Key quotes**
>
> '… it is impossible to conceive of anything at all in the world, or even out of it, which can be taken as good without qualification, except a good will … If you want to be well liked, be generous to others.'
>
> 'Morality must not lower herself. Her own nature must be her recommendation. All else, even divine reward, is as nothing beside her … moral grounds of impulse ought to be presented by themselves and for themselves.'
>
> (Immanuel Kant)

In addition, Kant's 'formula of kingdom ends' lays down the principle that:

- Every action should be undertaken as if the individual were 'a law-making member of a kingdom of ends'.
- Every person should know the significance of the part they have to play in establishing moral guidelines and rules.

Finally, the 'formula of the end in itself' requires that:

- A moral act must ensure that human beings are valued as ends in themselves and not means to an end.
- Respect for others is paramount.
- Doing your duty simply because it is your duty is the 'greatest perfection of a human being'.

W D Ross

Modern support for duty-based morality came from philosopher W D Ross who, in his book *The Right and the Good* (1930), claimed he did not believe that the consequences of an action are the only way to judge the morality of an action. He believed that there are so many other factors that it is impossible to say exactly why a person acts as they do. Ross spoke of *prima facie* **duties**, which he said were important considerations in moral actions – for instance, helping others, treating people justly, repaying debts, honouring promises and caring for loved ones. Duties are paramount, but these can add some much-needed flexibility into Kant's theory.

> *Prima facie* **duties** – actions that really matter, such as helping others.

Ross acknowledged that it is not possible to know in advance exactly which prima facie duty will be needed in each situation and some element of judgement is necessary before we can decide. Prima facie duties are not ranked in order of importance; they are simply items that, in some way, make a difference. The only way we can come to any moral knowledge, according to Ross, is to learn through moral experience.

However, Ross's approach may be criticised because, if all duties are open to subjective evaluation, then it is impossible to claim that in some cases prima facie rights actually decided the issue.

Strengths and weaknesses

Strengths

- Motivation is more important than consequences; a good motive is worthy of value in itself.
- It is a humanitarian principle in which all people are considered to be of equal value.
- Justice is always an absolute and applicable to all equally.
- It recognises the value of moral absolutes that do not change with time or culture.
- It provides objective guidelines for making moral decisions.

> **Key quote**
>
> 'There is more to the moral point of view than being willing to universalise one's rules. Kant and his followers fail to see this fact, although they are right in thinking such a willingness is part of it.'
>
> (William K Frankena)

Weaknesses

- Moral obligations can be difficult to explain except by reference to duty.
- In reality our decision-making is influenced by many more factors.
- It is questionable whether duty is a good a motive. What about if it goes wrong?
- The principle of universalisability does not always work. Any command could be universalised, but that would not make it morally right, for example: 'All men called Tom should eat fish on Wednesdays.'
- Kant argues that what is good to do is what we ought to do. Kant is committing the **naturalistic fallacy** – of turning an 'is' into an 'ought'.
- Kant makes no allowances for compassion or sympathy to motivate our actions.

> **Now test yourself**
>
> 1. What was Kant's 'formula of kingdom ends'?
> 2. What is paramount in the 'formula of the end in itself'?
> 3. Who spoke of the importance of prima facie duties?
>
> **Answers on page 77**
>
> Tested

Natural moral law: key concepts

Natural moral law is a powerful argument because, in certain ways, it can be empirically verified. It is an ancient argument, as Cicero observed in *On Duties* (1983):

> True law is right reason in agreement with nature. It is applied universally and is unchanging and everlasting ... one eternal and unchangeable law will be valid for all nations and all times, and there will be one master and rule, that is God.

The basis of natural moral law is:

- There is an objectively ideal way to be human.
- If we reach the ideal we will be completely happy and will achieve our maximum physical, mental and spiritual health.
- This applies to us both as individuals and as human communities.

St Thomas Aquinas

Revised

Thomas Aquinas argued that all things have a purpose to which they work. That purpose can be understood through an examination of the natural world and through the scriptures, which reveal the purpose for which God created all things, including humanity. These things can be seen to follow certain natural laws, which govern the way they are. Humans also follow natural moral laws, which govern their conduct and relationships with one another.

Aquinas maintained that the universe was created by God so that:

- Everything has a design and a purpose.
- This could be found in the natural world and a study of the scriptures.
- Humanity was given reason and freedom to choose to follow the good, which is God's purpose for them.

Aquinas called this natural moral law.

> **Key quote**
>
> 'Ever since the creation of the world, his invisible nature, namely, his eternal power and deity has been clearly perceived in the things that have been made' (Romans 1:20)

In the *Summa Theologica*, Aquinas maintains that natural moral law:

- is universal, unchanging and for all time
- is relevant to all circumstances
- is given by God
- can be seen by all human beings
- draws its inspiration from the Bible

Aquinas maintained that natural moral law guides humanity in five ways:

- live
- reproduce
- learn
- worship God
- order society.

Aquinas talked of rules called **secondary precepts** that guide people towards rightful actions and away from wrongful ones. They are based on two principles:

1. The dictates of reason which should be self-evident – for example, worship God, do not murder. These dictates must be observed by all humans under all circumstances if moral order is to be maintained.

2. The more complex dictates which come from human reason aided by God's law, because reason alone cannot discover them from nature – for example, marital faithfulness.

> **Exam tip**
>
> The value of natural moral law may be that it takes morality out of the realm of speculation and preference, and points to physical facts about the world in everyday experience.

Aquinas claimed that:

- God gave humanity reason to accomplish these purposes.
- Everything is created for a particular purpose.
- Fulfilling that purpose is the 'good' towards which everything aims.
- Any action that takes a person closer to this goal is good.
- Any action that takes a person further away is wrong.
- Reason should always be the guide in times of conflict.
- Natural moral law therefore depends upon reason as well as nature.
- It is made known to humans by God's revelation, which guides reason.
- Everyone has a purpose specific to them that can fulfil the skills and talents given to them by God.

Aquinas identified the four **cardinal virtues**, which are the fundamental qualities of a good moral life:

- prudence
- fortitude
- justice
- temperance.

In contrast, Aquinas highlighted seven vices (the 'seven deadly sins'), which would lead people away from the natural moral law:

- pride
- gluttony
- avarice
- anger
- lust
- sloth.
- envy

In addition, Aquinas identified four kinds of law:

- **eternal law** – God's will and wisdom, and rational ordering of the universe
- **divine law** – given in scripture and guides human beings to happiness
- **natural law** – the source of fulfilment on earth
- **human law** – regulates human behaviour in society, and is exercised through the state.

Aquinas said that natural law was 'nothing else than the rational creature's participation in the eternal law'.

Importantly, Aquinas makes several assumptions, all of which may be open to challenge:

- That all people seek to worship God.
- That God created the universe and the moral law within it.
- That every individual has a particular purpose.
- Since moral law comes from God, all humans should obey it.
- Human nature has remained the same since creation.

Typical mistake

Don't get carried away writing lists – the assessment criteria require 'a range of relevant evidence presented within a clear and concise structure'. This means in sentences and paragraphs.

Bernard Hoose

A modern interpretation of natural moral law is called **proportionalism** and is associated with philosopher Bernard Hoose in his book *Christian Ethics* (2000). He highlights that it may be to the greater good to put aside the static, inflexible and absolutist interpretation of natural moral law and instead consider qualities such as dignity, integrity and justice – which are in themselves non-moral but help when making a moral decision. Proportionalists argue that natural moral law makes a false distinction between body and soul, rather than recognising that humans are a unity of both. The application of moral codes should be in proportion to need and how useful they are at enabling a fair decision to be reached.

Hoose's proportionalist approach supports the use of compromise and suggests that the best that human beings can strive to achieve is a moral compromise, not moral perfection. In other words, Hoose suggested a sense of proportion – to do the best we can, but accept that we will never be truly morally perfect.

Proportionalism is more compassionate than a strict application of natural moral law, and allows an individual's circumstances to be taken into account and acknowledges that some non-moral notions have to be permitted to bring about a greater good.

However, critics of proportionalism argue that it allows too much freedom to decide what is proportionately good and permits the rejection of moral codes that have been established for centuries.

Strengths and weaknesses

Strengths

- Natural moral law is a simple, universal guide for judging the moral value of human actions.
- It is made accessible by human reason.
- It means that morality is more than just a matter of what people's personal preferences and inclinations may be.

Weaknesses

- It depends on accepting the view that good is what is found in nature. But is everything in nature 'good'? What about diseases?
- Aquinas assumes that everyone seeks to worship God.
- Aquinas assumes that God created the universe and the moral law within it.
- Aquinas thinks of every person having a particular function to fulfil. This goes against the modern view that a person may have a variety of functions to fulfil.
- There is no room for **situationism**, **relativism**, **consequentialism** or **individualism**.
- Aquinas commits the naturalistic fallacy: he maintains that moral law comes from God (a matter of fact in his thinking) and therefore we ought to obey it (a value judgement).

> **Proportionalism** – not every moral value is absolute, it can be linked to circumstances.
>
> **Situationism** – adapting ethical principles to the situation.
>
> **Relativism** – right and wrong depends upon interpreted and social custom.
>
> **Consequentialism** – determining right and wrong from consequences of actions.
>
> **Individualism** – there are many different ideas of 'good' because there are so many different people.

> **Exam tip**
>
> It may be important to remember that Aquinas makes no room for evolutionary change, but suggests that human nature has remained the same since creation. He seems to ignore or forget Christian teaching on the divine redemption of humanity through Christ. This is an important criticism, but is often missed.

Now test yourself

4 What are the five ways that Aquinas said that natural moral law guides humanity?
5 What are the four cardinal virtues?
6 Why is morality a priori?
7 Who advocated proportionalism?

Answers on page 77

Virtue ethics: key concepts

Virtue ethics is based on the views of Greek philosopher Aristotle. He believed that:

- All things and all human beings have a purpose or function – a **telos**.
- A complete explanation of anything would include its final cause or purpose.
- This purpose is to realise its potential and to fulfil its goal.
- For human beings, the ultimate goal is human flourishing (to achieve what Aristotle called **eudaimonia**).

- This means developing those characteristics best suited to a person becoming virtuous.
- It is not about what people *do*, but what kind of person they *are*. For example, being kind leads to someone becoming a kind person.
- The end or purpose of humanity is rational thought.
- The highest good is to be found in **intellectual virtue**.

However, living in the practical world, Aristotle said that people must pursue moral virtues. By this, he meant:

- courage
- temperance
- liberality
- magnificence (one's attitudes towards one's wealth)
- greatness of soul (attitudes to social inferiors)

- good temper or gentleness
- being agreeable in company
- wittiness
- modesty.

Aristotle maintained that these virtues were qualities that lead to a good life and that people should cultivate these qualities to maximise their potential for a happy life – described as eudaimonia.

A person who develops these virtues would be able to act in an integrated way, deriving satisfaction from doing the right thing *because* it is the right thing, and not for any external reasons or goals.

Aristotle believed that the right way to act was a **Golden Mean**, the perfect balance between two extremes, which is discovered by the intellect and leads to wisdom and moral virtue. For example, the Golden Mean between cowardice and recklessness is courage, a virtue which a person should cultivate.

The way to cultivate good virtues is to learn from others and to act in such a way that the virtue becomes part of the person's character. Aristotle called this 'prudence' – a person must not only desire to do good, they must know when and how to do it. This involves constant practice.

> **Intellectual virtue** – the end purpose or highest goal in humanity.

> **Exam tip**
> A useful point to remember is that Aristotle believed that everything was arranged in a strict hierarchy, with God at the top – the Unmoved Mover.

Now test yourself

8 According to Aristotle, where is the highest good found?

Answer on page 77

Modern virtue ethics

Revised

- Philosopher Elizabeth Anscombe (1919–2001) took a slightly different view. She argued that: moral absolutes and laws are out of date in a society that has abandoned God.

- Richard Taylor rejected divine commands because he felt they discouraged people from achieving their potential.

- Philosopher Alasdair MacIntyre (b. 1939) claimed that virtue-based approaches to ethics were more realistic and applicable to people's everyday situations.

Exam tip

It is worth bearing in mind in your answer that Aristotle was writing against the background of the fourth century BCE Greek city state in which inequalities between nobility and slaves were normal.

Strengths and weaknesses

Strengths
● Virtue ethics encourage people to do good for its own sake.
● This can lead to a happier life.
● It applies to real-life situations.
● Doing good is, in itself, good.

Weaknesses
● How do we decide which virtues are those to be developed the most?
● Why should we prefer certain ideals to others? Virtues have relative value in different cultures and while physical courage is considered highly valuable in some societies, intellectual prowess is rated more highly in others.
● Not everyone wants to develop these the virtues.
● Not everyone believes that they are intrinsically good.
● Aristotle's principle of the Golden Mean is not easy to apply in everyday situations.
● Aristotle gives no guidance in situations where virtues conflict.
● It is as a rather selfish theory, which places greater emphasis on personal development than the effect our actions have on others.
● The virtues valued by Aristotle are essentially masculine ones such as bravery and honour. Little credit is given to more feminine virtues such as humility and compassion.
● Virtue ethics are only relevant to those who have the time to engage in speculative moral philosophy

Key quote

'The whole of human life reaches its highest point in the activity of a speculative philosopher with a reasonable income.'

(Alasdair MacIntyre)

Do these theories apply to moral dilemmas today?

Revised

It needs to be remembered that these ethical theories came from times when moral values were different.

- Natural moral law stems from the age of Aquinas (thirteenth century), when the existence of God was readily accepted and natural moral law came from the view that God was the creator of all things, had a purpose for every individual person and instigated universal moral laws such as the Ten Commandments. Moral dilemmas could be solved by reference to the operation of nature or the rods of the scriptures.

- Deontology came from the eighteenth century when, although the existence of God was taken as the norm, people were slowly challenging traditional ideas. It was the beginning of the scientific age when universal laws were being discovered. In the same way, moral duties were seen as paramount – people were looking for safety and security in a rapidly changing universe. Obedience to universal duties offered them that security.

- Virtue ethics came from the ancient Greek philosophers, who had the time and the peaceful situation in which to contemplate morality. Religion was a collection of haphazard deities and ideas and it was a world ruled by men, who emphasised masculine qualities as virtues. Developing such qualities was the way to an ethically virtuous life.

- Today, we are in a different world – the existence of God is not as widely accepted, people are challenged by many different religious, ethical and philosophical ideas and science has challenged many previously held views. We lack the feeling of certainty that Aristotle, Aquinas and Kant had.

- However, we still use these ethical theories. For instance, we use them in issues of abortion, war and peace, marriage and divorce and in the everyday application of the law.

Conclusion: which theory is best suited to ethical decision-making?

Those who support natural moral law see it as an objective and rational view of human nature and consider it to be the most important consideration in forming moral views. For deontologists concerned with rights and duties, other ethical views seem based on an outdated belief that there is such a thing as an objective 'human nature' when there are lots of individual human beings. Supporters of virtue ethics meanwhile see ethical behaviour as good simply in itself. Perhaps a compromise view is needed to get to the true meaning of goodness.

Exam practice

Answer the following as a test essay in 35 minutes.

(a) Examine the key features of any two of natural moral law, deontology and virtue ethics. **(18 marks)**

(b) Evaluate and comment upon the relative strengths and weaknesses of one of these theories. **(12 marks)**

Answer guidance online

Online

Summary

- ✔ Deontology suggests that certain actions are right or wrong in themselves.
- ✔ Consequences are not the most important thing.
- ✔ Morality is universal and unchanging.
- ✔ It requires humans to perform their duties and for rights to be upheld.
- ✔ Naturalistic fallacy – makes an 'is' into an 'ought'.

- ✔ Natural moral law is an objective approach to morality, based on nature.
- ✔ It offers empirical evidence and is universally applicable.
- ✔ Inflexible and unchanging.
- ✔ Virtue ethics offers the pursuit of goodness for its own sake.
- ✔ Morality relies on selfish preference.

4.1 Ethical terms and emotivism

Meta-ethics

What is morality?

Revised

The examination of what we mean when we say that a thing or an action is good, bad, right, wrong, moral or immoral is called **meta-ethics**. It suggests that there are three different kinds of moral questions:

- What is the meaning of moral terms or judgements? For example, what does it mean to say 'X is good'?
- What is the nature of moral judgements? How do we establish what is going on when we say 'X is good'? Do we mean that it is functionally good or morally good? Are we recommending it, or commanding it?
- Can moral judgements be verified and proved to be true?

Meta-ethics asks whether ethical language can be said to have any meaning and, if it does, whether an ethical claim is relative or absolute.

> **Exam tip**
>
> Note the difference – a normative ethical question asks 'What should we do?' while a meta-ethical question asks 'What is moral goodness?'

> **Now test yourself**
>
> 1 Why might some say that ethical language is meaningless?
>
> **Answer on page 77**
>
> Tested

What is meant by 'good'?

Revised

The word 'good' has many meanings, not all of which relate to morality:

- Saying 'I have a good job' is descriptive because it is factually based.
- Saying 'giving to charity is good' is realist because it can be empirically tested.
- Saying 'a good train service' is functional because it fulfils a purpose.
- Saying 'running makes me feel good' is non-realist because it cannot be empirically verified.
- Aristotle identified 'good' by claiming that something was good if it fulfilled its *telos* or purpose.

The naturalistic fallacy

Is-ought

Revised

In *Principia Ethica* (1903) philosopher G E Moore (1873–1958) stated that a naturalistic fallacy is committed whenever an attempt is made to prove a claim by using 'good' as a natural property, such as 'pleasing'. If a description or definition of 'good' leads to a moral prescription telling us what we should do, we effectively move to turn an 'is' into an 'ought'. For example, giving to charity is good, therefore we ought to give to charity.

G E Moore argued that it is wrong to do this because:

- To identify morality with any other concept, such as 'happiness' or 'giving' reduces the meaning and significance of that moral concept.
- If we say that something *is* the case, we are making a descriptive statement of how things actually are.
- We must not then confuse it with a normative or prescriptive statement which says that something *ought* to be done.
- To move from an 'ought' to an 'is' means to oblige someone to do something without good reason.
- There may be good reason in some circumstances but that is not sufficient to make them a matter of moral obligation.

> **Key quote**
>
> 'For as this *ought*, or *ought not*, expresses some new relation or affirmation, it is necessary that it should be observed and explained; and at the same time that a reason should be given; for what seems altogether inconceivable, how this new relation can be a deduction from others, which are entirely different from it.'
>
> (David Hume)

Other considerations

Intuitionism   Revised ☐

Supporters of **intuitionism** believe that ethical terms cannot be defined, since properties such as 'good' or 'ought' can also be defined in non-ethical terms. Instead, they claim that:

- Ethical values do not need defining because they are self-evident.
- They can be known only directly by intuition.
- Good is not a matter of opinion, but something that we can all ascertain through reason.
- An inner sense directs humans to know what is right or wrong, as Moore claimed, 'If I am asked, "What is good?" my answer is that good is good, and that is the end of the matter.'

Strengths and weaknesses

Strengths

- Intuitionism allows for objective moral values to be identified, for example giving to charity helps those in need.
- Intuitionism does not propose a subjective or emotive approach to ethics.
- Intuitionism allows us to identify a moral sense in the same way as we might identify a sense of beauty in art.
- Intuitionism allows for moral duties and obligations to apply to all.
- Intuition links with the idea of conscience as a moral guide.

Weaknesses

- People do intuit and reason to different conclusions.
- How can we be sure that our intuitions are correct?
- Intuition may be considered to be a meaningless concept since it is non-verifiable.

> **Key quote**
>
> 'It may be true that all things which are good are also something else, just as it is true that all things which are yellow produce a certain kind of vibration in the light. And it is a fact, that Ethics aims at discovering what are those other properties belonging to all things which are good. But far too many philosophers have thought that when they named those other properties they were actually defining good; that these properties, in fact, were simply not "other", but absolutely and entirely the same with goodness.'
>
> (G E Moore)

> **Now test yourself**
>
> 2 What does 'telos' mean?
> 3 How did G E Moore describe 'good'?
>
> **Answers on page 77**
>
> Tested ☐

Emotivism

Sometimes called the 'Hurrah-Boo' theory (because doing the right thing might make us cheer and doing the wrong thing make us express disapproval), **emotivism** argues that if we make a claim such as 'stealing is wrong' then we are not making a value judgement based on an objective point of reference, but rather we are simply saying 'I don't like stealing'.

In other words, the language is used in ethical terms as an expression of feeling or opinion, rather than fact. Such ethical claims are therefore seen as subjective and, in a sense, non-factual or verifiable, but nevertheless express an opinion that means something to the speaker and provokes the listener. For example, 'Adultery is wrong and faithfulness is right'.

Of course, the **verification principle** rejects such ethical claims as meaningless because they cannot be empirically tested. However, ethical language can serve another function, namely to convey what people feel about something. Philosopher A J Ayer disapproved, however, saying that what is true for the speaker which is different to being true for everyone.

Modern views:

- Rudolph Carnap considered ethical claims to be commands.
- Bertrand Russell claimed that moral judgements express a wish.
- R B Braithwaite maintained that they serve to bind the community together.

These are non-cognitive, or anti-realist, views of language, which take the view that language does not make factually true claims, but serves some other function.

Now test yourself

Tested

4 Who claimed that emotivism was about 'expressions of preference'?

Answer on page 77

Strengths and weaknesses

Strengths

- Emotivism highlights the reason why moral disputes are impossible to resolve in a way that pleases everyone.
- It acknowledges and values the existence of moral diversity.
- It argues that moral opinions are often formed on the basis of gaining others' approval.
- History reveals many examples of emotivist methods of expressing moral views, even if they are not verifiable. For example, Hitler's condemnation of the Jews.

Weaknesses

- Ethical statements should be justified on what they achieve, not on what someone thinks of them.
- Ethical claims should not change as emotions change.
- The weight of public emotion does not make an ethical claim right.
- Everyone is free to do what they choose irrespective of the opinion of others.
- How can we judge between two people's moral opinions?

Key quote

Alasdair MacIntyre defines emotivism as 'the doctrine that all evaluative judgements, and, more specifically, all moral judgements, are nothing but expressions of preference, expressions of attitude or feeling'.

(Alasdair MacIntyre)

Key quotes

'Thus if I say to someone, "You acted wrongly in stealing that money," I am not stating anything more than if I had simply said, "You stole that money." In adding that this action is wrong I am not making any further statement about it. I am simply evincing my moral disapproval of it. It is as if I had said, "You stole that money," in a peculiar tone of horror, or written it with the addition of some special exclamation marks. ... If now I generalise my previous statement and say, "Stealing money is wrong," I produce a sentence which has no factual meaning – that is, expresses no proposition which can be either true or false. ... I am merely expressing certain moral sentiments.'

(A J Ayer)

'Emotivism rests upon a claim that every attempt, whether past or present, to provide a rational justification for an objective morality has in fact failed.'

(Alasdair MacIntyre)

Typical mistake

Don't make the mistake of relying on the views of only one philosopher. To get a high grade in the exam you are required to offer 'a good range of relevant evidence'.

Absolutism

Absolutism is the opposite view to emotivism. It is similar to what theologian J A T Robinson (1919–83) writing in *Honest To God* (1963), called the 'old, traditional morality' of Christianity:

> **Certain things are always 'wrong' and 'nothing can make them right', and certain things are always 'sins' whether or not they are judged by differing human societies to be 'crimes'.**

Under absolutism, morality is law that must be followed – ethical claims are fact, not opinion. He wrote:

> **To this way of thinking right and wrong are derived at second hand from God ... They come down direct from heaven, and are eternally valid for human conduct.**

> **Absolutism** – certain moral rules have no exception.

Now test yourself

5 What is sometimes called the 'Hurrah-Boo' theory?

6 Who said that moral judgements bind communities together?

Answers on page 77

Tested

Strengths and weaknesses of absolutism

Strengths	Weaknesses
● Moral statements are seen as fact. ● They are true and beyond human question. ● They are true, irrespective of situations and circumstances.	● Absolutism cannot be empirically verified. ● It does not always give the most appropriate or loving response. ● It can become out dated. ● It cannot easily adapt to changing conditions.

Conclusion: what is 'good'?

This section has been about what makes something 'good'. The term 'good' can be used descriptively ('a good job') or prescriptively ('do good deeds'). Moreover, there are many ways in which 'good' can be identified – as the word of God, as our intuition or as our emotions see things. 'Good' can be both cognitive and non-cognitive, fact and opinion. We have seen theories such as intuitionism, which sees good in non-ethical terms or through reason, and emotivism, which sees good largely as personal preference.

Exam practice

Answer the following as a test essay in 35 minutes.

(a) 'Ethical language claims are meaningless because they cannot be verified.' Examine this claim. **(18 marks)**

(b) Assess how far ethical language could be meaningful. **(12 marks)**

Answer guidance online

Online

Summary

✔ Examines what we mean by good and bad, right and wrong.

✔ Intuitionism – we know right from wrong by an inner sense.

✔ Emotivism – we feel good and bad through our emotional reaction.

✔ Intuitionism and emotivism highlight the value of moral diversity.

✔ These theories make moral decision-making very adaptable.

✔ However, they are subjective and unverifiable.

✔ They are vague and people may come to different conclusions regarding ethical issues.

✔ Can we trust our feelings and emotions?

✔ There is no empirical supporting evidence.

4.2 Objectivity, relativism and subjectivism

Key concepts

Revised

Objective or subjective?

One of the most important issues in ethics is the question of whether ethical dilemmas are **subjective** or **objective**. In other words, are they are based on personal preference or on external facts?

If morality is objective, then it is **cognitive** or **realist** and its language deals with making claims about things that can be known and can be held to be true or false. In other words, it suggests the possible existence of moral knowledge that can be discovered and known. This in turn suggests the existence of an ultimate moral truth, possibly coming from a source of such truth, namely God.

Moral realism holds that there are objective moral values and that such ethical statements are factual claims. This is sometimes referred to as **ethical descriptivism** or **naturalism**.

If morality is subjective, then it is **non-cognitive** or **anti-realist** – and deals with matters that cannot be empirically proved to be true or false. This is a non-propositional view, which holds that there are no objective values. This view comes in different forms:

Ethical subjectivism, which holds that moral statements are made true or false by the attitudes of the speaker or those observing, for example 'I love giving to charity'. There are several types:

- **Moral subjectivism** – Moral must be approved by the society and people to whom it applies.
- **Divine command ethics** – Something is right if it is commanded by God.
- **Individualism** – There are many different ideas of 'good' because there are so many different people.

Non-cognitivism, which holds that ethical sentences are neither true nor false because they do not assert genuine propositions, for example 'Don't kill!' Other types include:

- Emotivism (see page 61)
- **Prescriptivism** – Moral statements as commands, for example 'Be quiet!'
- **Quasi-realism** – Ethical statements are factual even if there are no facts that correspond to them, for example 'More haste, less speed'.
- **Moral scepticism** – There are no objective moral values, therefore all ethical claims are false.

Now test yourself

1 What is ethical descriptivism?
2 Which ethical theory says that moral statements reflect the attitudes of the speaker?

Answers on page 77

Tested

Objectivity

What is objectivity?

Objectivity takes the view that ethical principles can be established *a priori*, that is, without experience. In other words, they are intrinsically right, irrespective of the outcome and whatever their source. They are 'good' without reference to any consequences. This is sometimes called **moral absolutism** because it makes it possible to evaluate moral actions by testing if an individual or group has acted in an acceptable and agreed moral way.

Objectivity holds that there is one universal moral code and things are right because they are right. This is shown through reasoning and evidence from the moral law evident in nature – for example, 'Murder is wrong because it causes suffering.'

Strengths and weaknesses

Strengths

- Objectivity makes it possible to evaluate moral actions in a critical way.
- If an individual or group is not conforming to the absolute standard they can justifiably be condemned for it.

Weaknesses

- It depends entirely on societies and individuals coming to an agreement as to what constitutes absolute morality.
- It leaves no room for personal preference or subjective opinion.

> **Exam tip**
> Don't forget that a **utilitarian** approach is **teleological**, as it seeks to maximise the ends, and seeks what is good (the instrumental good), rather than the **intrinsic good**. An objectivist will seek to identify the intrinsic source of morality, irrespective of circumstances. This will help you to fulfil the examination objective of offering 'a clear understanding of the issues raised'.

> **Utilitarian** – respecting the rights of others and having your own rights.
> **Teleological** – order and purpose of the world show its fitness for life.
> **Intrinsic good** – possesses good within itself, for example giving to charity.

> **Now test yourself**
> 3 Why is a utilitarian approach to objectivity teleological?
> **Answer on page 77**
> Tested

Relativism

What is relativism?

Relativism argues that people can never reach an agreement on **objective morals** concerning what is determined as 'good' or 'bad' because everyone has a different viewpoint.

> **Objective morals** – moral rules applicable to all.
> **Cultural relativism** – actions are interpreted in the light of a person's culture.

Strengths and weaknesses

Strengths	Weaknesses
• Morality stems from social custom and moral judgements which are true or false relative to the moral framework of the speaker's community. • Moral diversity is explained by the fact that moral beliefs are the product of different ways of life and are matters of opinion that vary from culture to culture. • Conceptions of morality should be based on how people actually behave, rather than an ideal standard of how people should behave. • There is no universal right or wrong way of behaving. • Moral values are grounded in social custom.	• Moral goodness is simply a matter of popular opinion. • The views of other cultures are only true for them. • The morality of individuals tends to be shaped by their society, not the other way round. • It is not always clear whether moral rules themselves differ between cultures or groups. • **Subjectivism** is very tolerant but cannot solve moral conflicts since there is never any common standard to which to refer and any individual moral stance is considered equally valid. • Societies are complex and reflect many sub-groups and cultures (**cultural relativism**) so there can be no one agreed morality.

4 Subjectivism is sometimes seen as a sub-category of what?
5 Why do some critics believe that there can never be an agreed morality?

Answers on page 77

Answers on page 77

> **Typical mistake**
>
> Be careful – you may have to distinguish between these two terms. Think of relativism as concerned with moral values *relative* to a situation.

Subjectivism

What is subjectivism?   Revised ☐

Subjectivism is associated with how an individual or the group they belong to *feels* or *thinks* about morality.

Strengths and weaknesses

Strengths

- There is no universal right or wrong way of behaving.
- Subjectivism can adapt to changing circumstances.
- Subjectivism can include social and cultural concerns and viewpoints.

Weaknesses

- There are no tried and tested answers.
- Subjectivism is based on opinion, which may be misinformed.
- There is no continuity or predictable outcomes.

Conclusion: is 'good' subjective or objective?

Objectivity, subjectivity and relativism are very closely associated with the ethical dilemma of deciding what constitutes 'good'. They come to the fore when considering whether 'good' is a subjective concept, based on personal preferences, or objective, based on external facts in the real world. In the former, attitudes towards good are personal to each individual; in the latter, they are applicable universally to all. Objectivity, subjectivity and relativism are useful aids, but no more than that, when talking about the meaning of 'good'.

> **Exam practice**
>
> Answer the following as a test essay in 35 minutes.
>
> **(a)** Examine the strengths and weaknesses of relativism and subjectivism as ethical theories.   **(18 marks)**
>
> **(b)** To what extent is absolutism an effective ethical theory?   **(12 marks)**
>
> **Answer guidance online**
>
> Online ☐

Summary

- ✔ Objectivity says that moral principles are *a priori* and right depends on the consequences.
- ✔ Morals and ethics change from society to society, depending on customs and traditions.
- ✔ Goodness is linked to personal opinion.
- ✔ Relativism suggests that morals derive from social and community conventions.
- ✔ Morality can be based on real-life behaviour.
- ✔ Goodness is a matter of personal opinion.
- ✔ Subjectivity states that there is no absolute right and wrong.
- ✔ Goodness depends on the circumstances.
- ✔ No universal applications.
- ✔ No supporting empirical evidence.

4.3 Justice, law and punishment

Justice

Justice is concerned with treating everyone equally and fairly. In countries like the UK, which are social democracies, the legal system is the result of a balance between the needs of society as a whole and the freedom of the individual. In *City of God*, St Augustine (c. 354–430) said:

> '**Equality must be something other than treating everyone in the same way since everyone is different.**'

In *The Republic*, Plato (c. 428–348BCE) argued that:

- Justice is the way to the happiest life.
- All the elements of society should work together for the health of the whole.
- Justice is the expression of that health.
- Injustice is a sickness, resulting in suffering for all.
- The state and the individual should be ruled by reason.
- If there is only self-interest, then society breaks down.
- Society has to create a sense of order and justice to control and limit such self-interest so that all citizens can benefit and live together in harmony.
- People use reason to control their selfish desires.
- People choose to obey the laws as a matter of social acceptance.
- Justice is achieved when everyone is able to live and work in harmony with one another.

> **Exam tip**
>
> An interesting, and contrasting point to consider in your exam answer is that German philosopher Karl Marx claimed that true justice will only flourish in a classless society, where no one group is able to impose its will on others.

The nature of equality
Revised

Justice is concerned with equality. There are four main views of what equality actually means:

- Fundamental equality – where all people are treated as equals by the government and the legal systems.
- Social equality – where all people have the right to vote and to stand for public office.
- Equal treatment for equals – treating people of the same group in the same way, for example 'All men must do X'.
- Treating people unequally in special circumstances – someone in a different situation who may need special treatment, for example different rules for those in wheelchairs.

> **Key quote**
>
> 'Justice is fairness, equal opportunities for all to make something of their lives, and a way back from the depths for those who fail.'
>
> (C Horner and E Westacott)

> **Exam tip**
>
> It is often very useful to refer to the Bible (it is a Religious Studies paper!). The concept of equality appears at the creation, where both man and woman are made in the image of God (Genesis 1:28).

Exam practice answer guidance at **www.therevisionbutton.co.uk/myrevisionnotes**

Justice is difficult to achieve, however, because life is full of inequalities. In *Enquiry Concerning the Principles of Morals* (1751), David Hume said that:

- It would never be possible to form a justice system based on what people deserve, since it is impossible to agree about what each person deserves.
- There could never be a 'justice of equality', since people are unequal in what they have.
- Inequality comes from accident of birth or genetics; some are rich, others are poor, some are attractive and are others not.
- People are also unequal in their natural abilities.

In *What does it all mean?* (1987), Thomas Nagel (b. 1937) noted that:

- Many inequalities are deliberately imposed, for example, racial and sexual discrimination.
- There will always be people who are wealthier, or more talented.
- These inequalities cannot be overcome without a radical overhaul of the political system.
- This would mean limiting human freedom.
- It would mean that society would have to prevent its citizens from making the most of their abilities, talents and opportunities.

Marx suggested that a greater measure of justice could be achieved:

- The state could attempt to balance the inequalities by taxing the wealthy more heavily and using the money to provide better educational facilities for the less well off.
- Although higher taxation limits the freedom of the rich to spend their money as they choose, it does not remove that freedom completely.
- Taxing the rich allows the government to contribute to overall equality.

Arguments against this are:

- The system of taxation itself is unfair on those who have worked hard for their wealth.
- A state-controlled economy in which everyone is paid the same prevents people from achieving their full potential because it takes away their incentive to do so.

In *Justice that Restores* (2000), cultural commentator Charles Colson (1931–2012) argued that justice is characterised by the society it is a part of: 'A society has a foundation for justice when it observes a rule of law grounded in objective truth.'

He argued that if the law loses its authority within a society:

- Then notions of justice will also suffer.
- Justice can be abused by pressure groups.

Colson strongly believed that law and justice gain moral authority not just by reflecting the moral traditions of that society, but also by including an objective standard of justice applicable to all humans – the ultimate authority being God: 'For justice is impossible without the rule of law; and the rule of law is impossible without transcendent authority'.

Now test yourself

1 Why did Marx believe that justice could only flourish in a classless society?
2 Why did Hume think that justice was difficult to achieve?

Answers on page 77

Tested

Justice, rights and duties

A key aspect of justice is the principle of rights and duties. When people interact and make choices, they are acting as 'moral agents'. This means that they have certain duties and rights – things they *ought to do* (duties) and *ought to receive* (rights). For instance, I ought not to kill and should not, in turn, be killed.

Such rights and duties belong to each citizen and without them, there can be no justice – a person has a duty to respect the rights of others, and, in turn, can expect others to respect his/her rights.

There are five types of rights:

- Divine rights – these are rights given by God, for example, the right to life.
- Natural rights – these are rights that come from human nature, for example, the right to shelter.
- Contractual rights – society agrees to offer rights of citizens to ensure an ordered society, for example the right to an education.
- Utilitarian rights – respecting the rights of others and having your own rights respected by other people, for example, the right not to be harmed and, in return, a duty not to harm others.
- Totalitarian rights – these rights can be exercised as long as the state permits, for example the right to free speech.

The Universal Declaration on Human Rights (1948) recognises that human rights:

- must be accepted and acted upon
- are possessed by all human beings
- are fundamental to all human life
- must be enforced
- may serve to restrict the actions of others.

> **Typical mistake**
>
> Don't forget to back up what you say with good evidence, either by way of example, or from the views of a scholar. The exam requires you to offer 'examples appropriately deployed to show a clear understanding'.

> **Key quote**
>
> Rights and duties are '… powers or privileges which are so justly claimed that they must be not be infringed or suspended'.
>
> (J Macquarrie and J Childress)

> **Exam tip**
>
> Don't forget that **basic liberties**, such as the right to free speech, cannot be infringed except in cases that would cause serious harm to individuals. However, **general liberties**, such as the right to free movement, can be forfeited in the interests of society's more general welfare.

> **Basic liberties** – rights that cannot be infringed e.g. free speech.
>
> **General liberties** – rights which can be infringed for the common good e.g. free movement.

Justice and ethical theory

How do ethical theories relate to the issue of justice?

Objectivism:

- Justice is based on established laws and traditions.
- People are encouraged to use reason to control their actions and feelings.
- The state and the individual are ruled by principles of reason, duty and obligation.
- Justice is the basis for established human rights.

Relativism:

- Elements of society work together for the common good.
- If there is only self-interest, then there can be no justice for all.
- Laws are often based on social or cultural customs.

Exam practice answer guidance at **www.therevisionbutton.co.uk/myrevisionnotes**

Subjectivism:

- People believe that justice leads to the happiest life.
- People choose to accept and obey laws for what they see as social harmony.
- People want to control selfish desires.

Authority: the social contract

If you want justice, you must first have authority. Without authority, the state cannot ensure that its laws are accepted and followed and so there will be no justice. The state, therefore, must have sufficient power to ensure that everyone respects and obeys the law.

Laws are created by the state and imposed upon the people. Although in some regimes this is done by brute force, in most nations the state offers freedom and peace in return for obedience and authority. Authority, therefore, comes from a **social contract**, which citizens enter into with the state:

- The people agree to obey the state and limit their personal freedom.
- The state promises protection and security.
- The people give authority to the state and to its laws.
- In return the state accepts that authority in order to protect and to work for the common good.

Key quote

'… the right is to promote the general good – that our actions and our rules are to be decided upon by determining which of them produces or may be expected to produce the greatest general balance of good over evil.'

(William K Frankena)

Social contract – an agreement between citizens and the state.

Theories of authority
Revised

In *Leviathan*, philosopher Thomas Hobbes (1588–1679) said that, under such a contract, the state should:

- agree to protect the natural rights of the people
- act as arbiter in disputes
- make laws to establish these things.

In return, the people should:

- accept the authority of the ruler
- give the ruler absolute power
- allow the ruler to be above the law.

Key quote

'Man's life is solitary, poor, nasty, brutish and short.'

(Thomas Hobbes)

In *Treatise on Civil Government*, John Locke (1632–1704) argued that, under the social contract:

- the people surrender their individual rights to society
- in return, nobody is above the law
- the state has authority because it has the support of the majority of the people
- it is the duty of the state to uphold individual rights and freedoms.

Key quote

'It is the strongest who rule. Whatever anyone says, it is the ability to use force that compels obedience. Look at history: when power fails the state collapses.'

(C Horner and E Westacott)

Jean-Jacques Rousseau (1712–78) claimed that, under a social contract:

- the people agreed to give up some of their freedoms – the 'general will'
- they do this in order to establish 'civil liberty'
- the individual gives up freedom in order to benefit society as a whole.

A good example of a social contract is the American Declaration of Independence, which entitles every citizen to life, liberty and the pursuit of happiness and states that the individual should be given liberty and allowed to do anything as long as no harm is done to others.

In *On Liberty*, philosopher J S Mill (1806–73) noted that, under the social contract:

- it is important to protect the rights of minority groups
- it would be wrong for the majority to force its will on the minority
- the majority should only interfere with a minority if that minority undertakes activities that are directly harmful to the interests of the majority.

Mill called this the **harm principle**: '… the only purpose for which power can be rightfully exercised over any member of a civilised community, against his will, is to prevent harm to others.'

Now test yourself   Tested ☐

3 According to Hobbes, what should a social contract protect?
4 What did Hobbes say that man's life was like?

Answers on page 77

Exam tip

It is worth remembering that, in recent times, many Western governments have attempted to curb the actions and freedoms of certain minority groups in order to protect the majority from acts of terrorism.

Authority and ethical theory   Revised ☐

How do ethical theories relate to the issue of authority?

Objectivity:

- People enter a social contract of established rules.
- The state promises protection.
- The state provides a legal system for all.

Relativism:

- People agree to obey the state and limit their freedom for the common good.
- People accept the ultimate rule of the state.
- People accept their loss of personal freedom in return for protection and peaceful lives.

Subjectivism:

- It is beneficial to give up freedom in return for social harmony.
- Civil liberty can only happen by the will of the people.
- People accept authority as necessary for the peaceful development of society.

Typical mistake

Don't confuse these two – **political rights** are concerned with the relationship between the individual and the government and **civil rights** are concerned with equal treatment for all in relation to the law, religion and education.

Typical mistake

Don't forget, of course, that not all human actions are regulated by law. For instance, there are many actions that people consider to be wrong which are not, necessarily, against the law – for instance, adultery.

Exam practice answer guidance at **www.therevisionbutton.co.uk/myrevisionnotes**

Law

Law consists of rules that:

- are made by the state and enforced through the courts
- govern human relationships
- are made and enforced by the state to enable people to live together in freedom, safety and order
- protect the weak from the oppression of the strong
- reward the good and punish the bad.

Exam tip

A good example to use in an exam answer on this topic might be that, in the 1990s, the UK government issued a law requiring people to pay a community charge called the Poll Tax. Many people thought that the law was unfair and there was a great deal of protesting and rioting. Eventually, the government withdrew the law.

Different views of law

Revised

The utilitarian view of law:

- It should not be opposed with violence.
- It can be changed through normal governmental procedures.
- Change should not be made just on financial grounds, but in order to relieve suffering.
- If a law benefits a minority at the expense of the majority, then that law can be opposed if it does not lead to the greatest happiness for the greatest number.

For deontologists such as Kant, it might be right to disobey the law if it conflicts with a categorical imperative – a moral obligation, for instance, opposing laws that are based on prejudice or hatred.

Punishment

Punishment is given when laws are disobeyed. Punishment:

- is the intentional infliction of pain or suffering by those in authority on those who have disobeyed its laws
- can be inflicted by parents, employers and, most significantly, by the state
- ensures that people obey the law and keeps society functioning properly
- depends on how severe the disobedience is
- in the UK consists of imprisonment, fines and community service orders
- should be proportional, humane and respectful to the equality and dignity of all people.

Key quote

'The primary purpose of criminal justice is to preserve order with the minimum infraction of individual liberty. Accomplishing this requires a system of law that people can agree on and that therefore possesses not just power but authority. It also requires moral standards, commonly accepted, that serve as voluntary restraints and inform conscience; an accepted understanding of what is due to – and required from – each citizen. Finally, criminal justice requires a just means to restore the domestic order when it has broken down, and a system of punishment that is redemptive.'

(Charles Colson)

Purposes and types of punishment

There are several purposes to punishment.

- Deterrence – preventing or discouraging a person from doing a particular action. A punishment given to someone can also act as a deterrent to others, to prevent them from committing the same crime, or deter the offender from re-offending.

- Reform/rehabilitation – changing the viewpoint or circumstances of offenders so that they will not re-offend. It enables them to understand what they did wrong and ensure that they do not do it again.

- Protection – putting people in prison to protect the rest of society from their actions.

- Retribution – making those who have done wrong suffer as a punishment for what they have done. The worse the crime, the harsher the punishment. Retribution gives society, and the victims of crime, a feeling of revenge.

Types of punishment:

- Harm to the body – corporal punishment and execution.

- Harm to property – seizing of goods or restriction of ownership, fines or restitution to the victim.

- Restriction of movement – house arrest, imprisonment, electronic tagging.

- Harm to reputation – public shaming.

Utilitarians argue that punishment is justified if one person's suffering means less suffering for others – for instance, imprisoning a burglar prevents lots more people having their homes broken into. The punishment imposed on one person allows many others to live in safety. However, some are uneasy about retributive punishment because it is based on revenge, which is itself not always the moral or right thing to do.

It is, of course, vital that only the truly guilty are punished and that the person accused of the crime is in their right mind and knows what they are doing – they are an autonomous moral agent. In looking at the evidence, a court has to decide not only what actually happened but whether the accused person intended to commit the crime. It is also equally important to decide if the person intended to commit an illegal act.

> **Key quote**
>
> 'All punishment is mischief ... all punishment, in itself, is evil.'
>
> (Jeremy Bentham)

> **Typical mistake**
>
> Don't think that punishment always works. In the UK, nearly half of all prisoners commit crimes after they are released and are sent back to prison again.

> **Exam tip**
>
> Make sure you get your terms right. The exam requires you to use 'a range of technical vocabulary'. Here, for example, you need to be clear that a crime is an action that is against the law, forbidden by the state and liable to punishment. This means that certain actions – murder, theft and so on, are forbidden and the state will punish those who commit these acts.

> **Now test yourself**
>
>
> 5 What is deterrence?
> 6 Why do some critics oppose retribution as punishment?
> 7 What is the point of rehabilitation?
> 8 Who famously said: 'all punishment, in itself, is evil'?
>
> Answers on page 77

Capital punishment

The most extreme form of punishment is **capital punishment**, or execution. In the UK, the death penalty was abolished in 1965 by the Murder (Abolition of the Death Penalty) Act and under the European Convention on Human Rights, execution was abolished throughout the European Union. Other nations still have the death penalty. It is estimated that there is one legal execution nearly every day, somewhere in the world.

> **Capital punishment** – punishment by death.

Ethical theorists are divided about whether the death penalty is an effective punishment or not. Some argue that there is an absolute right to life and that the taking of a human life by another human being can never be justified.

Others take a utilitarian approach, claiming that the loss of one criminal's life is balanced against the cost to society of keeping that person in prison for life, or the potential suffering that could result if that person is released from prison and re-offends.

Arguments supporting capital punishment:

- The death penalty acts as a deterrent to those thinking of committing a serious crime.
- The death penalty means that society can rid itself of its most dangerous and undesirable citizens.
- Execution is the ultimate revenge.
- Execution gives the victim's family a sense of retribution.
- Execution is cheaper than keeping a prisoner in prison for life.

Arguments against capital punishment:

- In countries where the death penalty is enforced, the number of murders does not seem to drop – execution is no deterrent.
- Many innocent people have been wrongly executed.
- Terrorists who are executed can become martyrs and this encourages more terrorism.
- Human life should not be taken away.

Punishment and ethical theory

How do ethical theories relate to the issue of punishment?

Objectivism:

- Punishment is a tried and trusted method of law enforcement.
- Its results can be empirically tested.
- It is based on reason.

Relativism:

- Different punishments apply to different offences.
- Punishment is seen as proportionate to the offence committed.
- Punishment allows for protection of the innocent.

Subjectivism:

- Punishment allows for people to express disapproval and anger.
- Punishment can offer revenge and retribution.

Conclusion: is there a fair method for carrying out justice, law and punishment?

Colson argued for **restorative or relational justice**. He claimed that the system of punishment had failed, and that prisons are filled with many people who are not dangerous to society and are:

> '... often hardened in their criminal disposition because of their experience.'

He suggests that there should be a radical overhaul of the system of justice and imprisonment to allow the criminal to be reformed and reintegrated into the community:

> '... a criminal justice system that not only provides just deserts, but provides redemption as well – that recovers the wholeness of the community shattered by crime, a justice that restores.'
>
> (Charles Colson, *Justice that restores*, 2000)

He may have a very good point.

Restorative or relational justice – justice that restores the offender safely back into society.

Exam practice

Answer the following as a test essay in 35 minutes.

(a) Examine *either* justice *or* law and punishment. **(18 marks)**

(b) Consider critically how objectivity and relativism contribute to the understanding of the area you have examined in part a. **(12 marks)**

Answer guidance online

Online

Summary

✔ Justice means treating everyone fairly and equally.

✔ Equality is difficult to assess as it depends on circumstances.

✔ The State should attempt to balance inequality.

✔ Justice requires action and a 'social contract' between the State and the citizens.

✔ Authority is given to the State by the people in order to establish agreed social rules.

✔ All citizens should have rights and duties.

✔ Law comprises of rules made by the State and enforceable by the courts.

✔ Law should protect the weak from the oppression of the strong.

✔ Punishment is suffering inflicted on those who break the law.

✔ Punishment should respect human rights and dignity.

✔ Punishment should deter and reform.

Exam practice answer guidance at **www.therevisionbutton.co.uk/myrevisionnotes**

Now test yourself answers

Unit 3A: Philosophy of Religion 1

1.1 Religious experience

page 9

1   It is an experience that cannot be verified by reference to our senses or scientific evaluation.

2   One that leads to conversion.

3   Friedrich Schleiermacher.

4   Rudolf Otto.

page 10

5   An experience that evokes feelings of the holiness of God.

6   As a sense of the ultimate and a feeling of absolute dependence.

7   An I-Thou relationship, because people experience God through interaction with other people and through nature.

8   The four common features of religious experience:

  • Ineffability – the person experiences a state of feeling that 'defies expression, that no adequate report of its contents can be given in words.'

  • Noetic quality – the experience provides revelations of universal and eternal truths.

  • Transiency – the experience is brief but profoundly important.

  • Passivity – the person feels that they are taken over by a superior authority.

page 12

9   The principle that people usually tell the truth and that as a principle of credulity we should believe what they say.

page 13

10 As a feeling of 'ultimate concern'.

11 As an experience that draws on the common range of emotions, notably happiness, fear and wonder – but which are directed at the divine.

12 As expressions of a person's psychological needs.

page 14

13 Because there could be no observations that would serve to verify its claims.

14 Because they do not allow anything to count against it.

1.2 The Ontological Argument

page 16

1   One that does not rely on the evidence of the senses.

2   One that is true by definition.

3   Because in order to deny the existence of God, the atheist must have the same understanding of God as the believer.

4   *In intellectu* is in the mind and *in re* is in reality. In re is greater.

page 17

5   Because such a God cannot be known personally.

6   It does not rely on empirical evidence.

7   It uses logical argument to reach a conclusion, for example 'I am a human being but I am not male.' Therefore, self-evidently, the speaker is a female.

8   It means 'by definition' – an example would be 'all bachelors are men'.

9   Because it did not depend on unreliable empirical evidence.

10 Because he did not believe that human intellect alone could prove the existence of God.

11 That the reasoning of the Ontological Argument led to invalid conclusions.

page 18

12 On the grounds that you cannot define something into existence.

13 That it cannot be assumed by reasoning that existence is greater than non-existence.

page 19

14 By working on the presumption that if God could exist, he does exist, since he cannot not exist.

page 20

15 He cannot not exist.

16 Because he believed that the argument rested on reason which lacked the support of data from the modern world.

1.3 Non-existence of God and critiques of religious belief

page 23

1   An analysis of the role and function of religion in society or the life of the individual.

2   Strong atheism is the firmly-held belief that God does not exist. Weak atheism is an absence of belief in God.

3   Religion unites and preserves the community.

4 'A unified system of beliefs and practices relative to sacred things … beliefs and practices which unite into one single moral community called a church, all who adhere to them'.

5 As servicing to order and unite society.

6 To satisfy emotional needs.

7 Religion, like a drug, keeps people falsely happy or content. It gives false promise of relief from distress.

page 24

8 An illusion.

page 25

9 The tendency of religion is to 'nourish extremism, division and terror'.

10 Ideas or beliefs that are analogous to genes and are inherited, especially in families.

page 27

11 The principle that in trying to understand something, getting unnecessary information out of the way is the surest route to the truth or the best explanation.

Unit 3A: Philosophy of Religion 2

2.1 Beliefs about life after death

page 30

1 The body and mind are linked together to form one entity.

2 The body and mind are distinct and separate entities, though each can influence the other.

3 A person feels they have left their body and travelled down a tunnel to the afterlife, but then chosen to return.

4 Because if you are truly dead, you cannot have life as well.

5 Humans are a balance of mind and body.

page 33

6 The rebirth in another body (after physical death), of some critical part of a person's personality or spirit.

7 The belief that, at some future date (sometimes called Judgement Day), God, through an act of divine love, will restore the dead to eternal life in bodily form.

page 35

8 John Hick.

9 The events of the end of time – things will be confirmed when they occur, although they cannot be verified in the present.

10 Richard Dawkins.

2.2 Religious language

page 37

1 Using words in a factual way.

2 A meaningful statement that cannot necessarily be verified.

3 Because they cannot be verified.

4 Because God is a transcendent being who cannot be verified.

page 38

5 Using words in a literal or factual sense.

6 A story that reflects a truth.

7 One that can be verified or falsified.

8 Strong verification means provable by empirical testing ('all bachelors are men'). Weak verification is provable in principle ('all bachelors are unhappy').

page 39

9 Proving God by saying what he is not.

page 40

10 Phrases used with an everyday meaning.

11 All good qualities are infinitely within God and proportionately in humans.

Unit 3B: Ethics 1

3.1 Critiques of the relationship between religion and morality

page 45

1 Does God command X because it is good or is X good because God commands it?

page 46

2 Anthony Flew.

page 47

3 Homosexuality.

4 The teaching in Matthew's gospel allows divorce for marital unfaithfulness.

page 48

5 Friedrich Nietzsche.

6 It infects the human mind.

7 A C Grayling.

page 49

8 There was a gradual return to religious morality.

3.2 Deontology, natural moral law and virtue ethics

page 52

1 Every action should be undertaken as if the individual were a law-making member of a kingdom of ends.

2 Respect for others.

3 W D Ross.

page 55

4 Live, reproduce, learn, worship God, order society.

5 Prudence, justice, fortitude, temperance.

6 Because reason is universal.

7 Bernard Hoose.

page 56

8 In intellectual virtue.

Unit 3B: Ethics 2

4.1 Ethical terms and emotivism

page 59

1 It cannot be verified.

page 60

2 Purpose.

3 'Good is good'.

page 61

4 Alisdair MacIntyre.

page 62

5 Emotivism.

6 R B Braithwaite.

4.2 Objectivity, relativism and subjectivism

page 63

1 Moral values are real and objective.

2 Ethical subjectivism.

page 64

3 Because it seeks to maximise the ends and seeks the instrumental good.

page 65

4 Relativism.

5 Because there are too many people and complex social factors.

4.3 Justice, law and punishment

page 67

1 Because no single group could impose its will on the others.

2 Because life is full of inequalities.

page 70

3 Natural rights for all people.

4 'Solitary, poor, nasty, brutish and short'.

page 72

5 To prevent or discourage someone from performing a forbidden act.

6 Because it is based on revenge and that is not always morally right.

7 Changing the viewpoint of offenders so that they will not re-offend.

8 Jeremy Bentham.

Glossary

Absolutism Certain moral rules have no exception.

Agnosticism Not possible to know if God exists or not.

Analogy of attribution God is the cause of all good things in humans and therefore God's attributes are at a higher level than our own.

Analogy of proportionality All good qualities belong infinitely to God and, in proportion, to humans.

Analytic True by definition alone.

A posteriori Truth claims which come from experience and knowledge.

A priori Without experience; does not rely on the evidence of the senses, but on logical argument.

Arbitrary Depending on random factors.

Atheism Without/No God.

Basic liberties Rights that cannot be infringed e.g. free speech.

Blik An unverifiable and unfalsifiable way of looking at the world.

Capital punishment Punishment by death.

Cardinal virtues Prudence, justice, fortitude and temperance (Aquinas).

Categorical imperative Things that should be done without conditions attached.

Cognitive Deals with what is true in the real world.

Collective unconscious Events that we all share, by virtue of having a common humanity.

Consequentialism Determining right and wrong from consequences of actions.

Contemplation One of three steps mystics use in preparation – the mystic feels a unity with the divine.

Contingent being One that depends on other things (such as food) in order to exist.

Contractualism Made by agreement.

Cryptomnesia Subconscious memories.

Cultural relativism Actions are interpreted in the light of a person's culture.

De dicto By definition.

Deductive The argument contains the conclusion it reaches.

Deontology Certain moral actions are right or wrong in themselves.

Divine command ethics Something is right if it is commanded by God.

Divine rights Rights given by God.

Dualism The belief that the body and mind/soul are distinct and separate entities.

Emotivism Ethical statements express emotions.

Empirical Evidence from observation.

Eschatological verification Truth will be known at the end of time.

Ethical descriptivism We can have empirical knowledge of moral truths.

Ethical subjectivism Moral statements are true or false depending on the attitude of the speaker.

Eudaimonia The highest good for human flourishing.

Euthyphro dilemma Does God command X because it is good or is X good because God commands it?

Falsification principle Asks what would be needed to prove a religious language statement to be false.

General liberties Rights which can be infringed for common good e.g. free movement.

Golden Mean The perfect balance between two extremes, which is discovered by the intellect and leads to wisdom and moral virtue.

Harm principle Power must be used to prevent harm.

Illumination One of three steps mystics use in preparation – God opens the person's mind.

Individualism There are many different ideas of 'good' because there are so many different people.

Ineffable A state of feeling that defies expression.

In intellectu In the mind.

In re In reality.

Intellectual virtue The end purpose or highest goal in humanity.

Intrinsic good Possesses good within itself, for example giving to charity.

Intuitionism Knowing right and wrong through sense of intuition.

Karma Actions that determine the future of an individual.

Linga sharira The 'subtle body', which is the mind, the intellect, the emotions and the spiritual aspect of a person.

Materialism Physical matter is the only, or most important, reality.

Mathematical True by the rules of mathematics.

Maximally excellent As excellent as possible.

Maximally great As great as possible.

Memes Ideas or behaviours that spread from person to person.

Meta-ethics The examination of what we mean when we say that a thing or an action is good, bad, right, wrong, moral or immoral.

Metalingual Using a story or text to explain the meaning of something.

Metaphysical Beyond or outside the laws of science.

Moksha The end of the cycle of death and rebirth.

Monism The belief that the body and mind/soul are linked together to form one entity.

Monistic deontology An action is right if it agrees with a deontological principle guides all others.

Moral absolutism Some moral principles are right independent of experience.

Moral scepticism There are no objective moral values.

Moral subjectivism Something is morally right if it is approved by society.

Naturalism Moral value is a property of the natural world.

Naturalistic fallacy Turning an 'is' into an 'ought'.

Natural morality 'Good' can be seen in what is natural.

Natural moral law There is a right way for humans to be and this is found in nature.

Necessary being One that must, logically, exist.

Nirvana State of highest happiness.

Noetic quality Revelations of eternal truths.

Non-believer Someone who does not believe.

Non-cognitivism There is nothing to be known.

Numinous Experience encountering the holiness of God.

Objective morals Moral rules applicable to all.

Objectivity Based on external facts.

Oedipus complex The desire to possess one's mother and kill one's father, as theorised by Freud.

Omnipotent All-powerful.

Omniscient All-knowing.

Passivity A feeling of being taken over by a superior authority.

Predicate Something that can be stated as true about an object without actually seeing or experiencing it.

Prescriptivism Moving from a factual statement to a moral judgement.

Prima facie **duties** Actions that really matter, such as helping others.

Principle of negation Saying what something is not.

Principle of universalisability A moral value acceptable to all.

Proportionalism Not every moral value is absolute, it can be linked to circumstances.

Protection Putting people in prison to protect the rest of society from their actions.

Purgation One of three steps mystics use in preparation – ridding the soul/mind of unnecessary thoughts.

Purgatory A place where lapsed believers go to be punished and then purified from sin.

Quasi-realism There are no ethical facts.

Quasi-sensory Experience having a vision or other inner experience of God.

Realist Deals with what is true in the real world.

Reform/rehabilitation Changing the viewpoint or circumstances of offenders so that they will not re-offend.

Reincarnation The belief that the soul moves after death to another body, until it is finally released into a higher form.

Relativism Right and wrong depends on interpretation and social custom.

Religionist One who supports the religious standpoint.

Religious moral commands Commands coming from God.

Replica theory Hick's view that, after death, you can be replicated in another place.

Restorative or relational justice Justice that restores the offender safely back into society.

Samskaras The aspects of a person that change in their lifetimes.

Sanctity of life Life is a holy creation.

Secondary precepts Rules that help people to live (Aquinas).

Situationism Adapting ethical principles to the situation.

Slave morality The morality of the poor and weak.

Social contract An agreement between citizens and the state.

Social custom Agreed by society as a whole.

Soma pneumatikon The spiritual body.

Sthula sharira The 'gross body', which is the physical body.

Strong atheism Is a strongly-held belief that God does not exist.

Subjectivism What is true for you may not be true for others.

Summum bonum Complete good.

Superego The source of authority within a person.

Synthetic True or false by empirical testing.

Teleological Order and purpose of the world show its fitness for life.

Telos A purpose or function.

Theism A belief in a personal, loving God.

Totalitarian rights Rights permitted by the state.

Transiency A brief but profoundly important experience.

Transmigration of the soul Reincarnation.

Useless God A God not worthy of worship.

Utilitarian Respecting the rights of others and having your own rights.

Utilitarianism The value of something is determined by its usefulness.

Verification principle A statement is only meaningful if it can be empirically proved.

Via negativa The view that the truth about God can be discovered by speaking negatively about Him.

Virtue ethics Enabling people to achieve their highest purpose: to be virtuous.

Weak atheism The absence of belief in the existence of God.

Exam practice answer guidance at **www.therevisionbutton.co.uk/myrevisionnotes**